Ira Seymour Dodd

The Song of the Rappahannock

Sketches of the Civil War

Ira Seymour Dodd

The Song of the Rappahannock
Sketches of the Civil War

ISBN/EAN: 9783337008192

Printed in Europe, USA, Canada, Australia, Japan

Cover: Foto ©ninafisch / pixelio.de

More available books at **www.hansebooks.com**

The Song
Of the Rappahannock

Sketches of the Civil War

By

Ira Seymour Dodd

New York

Dodd, Mead and Company

1898

University Press:

JOHN WILSON AND SON, CAMBRIDGE, U.S.A.

TO MY COMRADES

The Living and the Dead

THESE MEMORIES OF OUR DAYS OF WARFARE
ARE AFFECTIONATELY DEDICATED

Preface

WHAT is herein written was begun and for the most part completed before the Spanish War Cloud was more than a distant and doubtful threat.

But out of its passing storm a rainbow arch has risen, fairer and sweeter than even the sunshine of victory to the eyes of those who stood in opposing ranks as foemen thirty years ago. We learned, not hatred, but profound respect for each other on those grimly fought fields of Civil Strife. During these years of retrospect and reflection the respect has been ripening into a warmer feeling; and now our hearts swell with deep and solemn thankfulness for the open evidence of our perfect welding into One Mighty Nation under whose Old Flag men of the South stand joined with men of the North in invincible brotherhood.

Henceforth memories of that older crisis can no longer be dividing or exclusive possessions, but each fragment of its story becomes part of the common heritage of American manhood.

To the kindness of the Editors of "McClure's Magazine," in which several of the sketches composing this little book first appeared, the author desires to express his obligations.

I. S. D.

RIVERDALE ON THE HUDSON
October 1, 1898.

Contents

The Song
of the Rappahannock

THE Song has been silent for more than thirty years. In another thirty years it will cease to be a living memory save to a handful of very old men. But those who once heard can never forget its weird, fantastic, sinister tones. Sometimes it was a fearful yet persuasive whisper addressed to you personally ; again it would burst in uncontrolled passion into a chorus of awful and discordant screams mingled with thunderous and reverberating roar. With marvellous range of tone and expression it was, however, always one Song with one fateful burden.

I was a young soldier of the Army of the Potomac in those days; one of the several thousand who wore the white cross of the Second Division of the Sixth Army Corps, and the Song in all its variations became a familiar sound.

For instance, once when we were occupying the hills north of the Rappahannock, nearly half the regiment were on the sick list by reason of the bad water which supplied our camp. Down by the river bank, perhaps a mile and a half away was a spring of good clear water. "Joe" and myself, both non-commissioned officers, thought we must at all hazards keep fit for duty, and on alternate mornings one of us would make the trip to fill our canteens. Wide and open fields lay between us and the spring and I think I never crossed that open space without hearing the Song. Preceding a distant detonation from beyond the river a faint quavering whistle would come, growing louder as with apparently increasing hurry it drew near. It seemed to speak in fascinating, insinuating tone of some very special message to you alone; then suddenly, with venomous buzz in your very ear while your heart stood still it would speed by and die away again in the farther distance. It was the voice of a minié bullet from the rifle of some sharpshooter on the Confederade picket line. But the range was long, the risk slight, as such things went, and not to be compared, so Joe and I thought, to the very real danger of the camp water.

Toward evening one of our field batteries would gallop down to the river bank and open fire upon those troublesome sharpshooters; then the heavy guns on the other side would make reply and a new variation of the

Song would be heard — a very Wagnerian orchestral effect : the quick crack of the field guns, the more distant boom of the siege cannon, the scream of shells rushing hither and thither through the evening air, always with that rising and falling cadence, that mournful moan, that peculiar hurrying, threatening, almost speaking quaver which, once heard goes with you evermore, so that years afterwards you hear it in your dreams.

Those big shells from the enemy's guns three miles away made regular evening visits to our camp. They seldom did any real harm. When we first occupied the position, a few tents were pitched too near the crest of the hill within sight of the gunners beyond; but after one of those tents had been torn to rags and the head of a poor fellow standing near had been neatly shorn off, everything came down behind the slope out of view; and though we were always favoured with our vesper serenade and close calls were not uncommon, no one else, I think, was seriously hurt.

The evening performance had, if not an appreciative, certainly a grimly critical audience. A veteran in the adjoining regiment calmly proceeds with the all-important business of boiling his coffee until a shell explodes uncomfortably close. Then you hear his disgusted growl: "The damned rascals! They spoil my supper every night!" and the answering jeer of his comrades: " Jim, did you hear what that one said? It said, ' Which 'un, which 'un, which 'un, *you!* ' "

The ring of the bursting shells was not the least impressive of the notes of the Song. It is hard to describe; but strange as it may seem to say so it was certainly music, often with absolutely sweet tones like the sudden stroke of a bell, followed by the singing hum, in curious harmony of the rushing of jagged iron fragments through the air. One of the friends of my boyhood was a musical genius, a pianist of no mean power who had studied his profession in Germany. The democratic make-up of our army is illustrated by the fact that, in the early sixties this man enlisted as a private soldier. And he used to amuse himself while lying in the trenches by noting the varying keys of the music of moaning and bursting shells.

But the Song was not always harm-less or ineffectual. No one knows precisely how many men suffered wounds and death beside the banks of the pretty, placid Rappahannock. It is within bounds to put the number at fifty thousand. The war history of that region is peculiar. It is a tale of incessant and resultless strife, seldom without at least the intermittent fire of opposing picket lines. Three of the greatest, most deadly, yet most indecisive battles of the war were fought there.

The veil of time has begun to fall over the actual agonies of the nation while the fury of that great war tempest lingered; but some of us remember how real it was, and the Song of the Rappahannock seems its very voice. It was Delphic in the ambiguity of its utterance. Neither the pæan of victory nor the wail of the conquered, it was the breath of the Titanic struggle with its bitter pain, its dark suspense, its grim and terrible stress and strain.

In early May, that sweet season when in Virginia springtime is just passing into summer, we came to the banks of the Rappahannock, ready to take our destined share in the battle of Chancellorsville. The river was no stranger : we had formed its intimate acquaintance in December during the bloody days of Fredericksburg ; and now, separated from the main body of the army which had crossed about fifteen miles above, we found ourselves once more facing the old battle-ground with its familiar sleepy town, its wide fields and amphitheatre of gentle hills spread out in portentous panorama before us. Peace seemed to have settled down upon the scene, blotting out all memory of strife ; yet we knew the semblance was but a mocking phantasm, for our comrades of the First Corps stirred up a very hornet's nest of enemies and had a sharp brush before they could lay their pontoon bridge. And though with this exception the Song was ominously silent in our front, we could hear its distant voice from up the river.

On one day it rose into an angry roar, and immediately afterward the First Corps received marching orders, went filing past us along the river road toward the sound of the Song, and the Sixth was left alone. On Saturday night our time came. It was a lovely evening full of the breath of spring-time; but our hearts were very solemn as, in the darkness and in sternly enforced silence our lines crept across the pontoon bridge out into the fields full of the ghosts of December's awful sacrifices and finally, with rifles loaded and with battle provision of sixty rounds of cartridge to every man, we halted before the spectral outlines of the Fredericksburg hills.

Then in low tones the order passed from company to company: " Lie down where you are. Let every man keep his gun by his side. Do not take off any of your equipments; do not even loosen your belts.   Keep silence!"

A battery moves like a group of shadows out a little way to the front; we can hear the subdued orders of the officers, the unlimbering and loading of the guns, and then all is quiet along the Rappahannock.   Beyond the guns we know there are pickets whose duty it is to wake and watch; but soon all along the inner lines the May moon shines peacefully on rows of sleeping men.   By to-morrow night many of them will lie very quiet in another and a deeper sleep.

Dawn comes soon in May, and the first gray light brought the Song. With hum and buzz like that of ghostly insects the bullets came stealing over from the enemy's skirmish line.   It was a grim awakening and its first impression inexpressibly mournful.   Each singing bullet seemed to chant a dirge — and the morning air held a very graveyard chill. Swearing is a common dialect with soldiers, but not an oath was heard as that morning Song began. Everyone was solemn; we were thinking of home and of loved ones, and there was a great despairing sense of separation in our hearts. I think almost any man who has seen war would tell the same story and count those moments of the skirmish firing in the gray dawn on the brink of battle among the most gloomy of his life.

But hark! The batteries are opening fire, the Song is bursting into fuller voice; and up and down the line orders ring out sharply, "Attention, battalion!" There is movement now, it brings life and dispels the gloom. There is marching and countermarching for better position and soon the line is placed in a sunken road whose banks protect us against the enemy's shot and shell, while just behind, on slightly higher ground our own batteries fire over our heads. And so the morning passes; the Song, never silent sometimes swells out clamorously; and anon it sinks to intermittent growls.

Suddenly, about noontime, there is a restless movement along the line; staff officers are galloping furiously hither and thither; something is in the air. We are ordered to unsling our knapsacks and pile them together. Meantime our batteries open a furious fire. The men say to each other, "The bulldogs are barking, and our turn is coming!" And as the Song swells with their baying, by quick orders our line is formed for the charge. We must storm those hills flaming with the fire of the Confederate cannons. A few breathless moments that seem like hours, and suddenly our batteries cease fire, the expected order is given, and the line surges forward.

I make no attempt to tell how the Sixth Corps on that Sunday morning won the Fredericksburg heights, storming successfully though with fearful loss, the very same works from which the army had been beaten back in December.

I am not a military critic, I can tell only what one very young and obscure soldier saw and felt.

I was a serjeant, and on that day my especial duty was that of " left general guide." The regiment was comparatively new and raw, and in our rush across the rough ploughed fields under the awful fire of the enemy's batteries we were thrown into some confusion. With great presence of mind our lieutenant-colonel halted us, ordered

the men to lie down, and then called
for "guides on a line." That meant
that I and the two other guides, one on
the right and one in the centre, were to
stand up and take position by which the
regiment could align itself. I sprang
to my feet, soon caught the line from
the others, and there we stood while
the regiment crawled up and " dressed "
by us. It was a trying situation ; and
the Song ! it was deafening. The air
was full of wild shrieks of grape and
shrapnel ; the ringing shells were bursting all about with maddening and stun-
ning detonations. I remember, as I
stood there for those few moments I
seemed indeed to have lost all sense
of fear, and yet I wondered whether
I was actually myself and whether my
head was really on or off my shoulders.

Then, as we raced forward once more
and neared the enemy's position, I remember that at regular intervals bul-

lets would strike close to my feet and
throw stinging little showers of gravel
in my face. I thought little of it at
the time, but among the prisoners captured were some sharpshooters who
had been posted off at our left; and
when I heard how those fellows had
bragged about the number of shots
they had fired at individual officers in
our regiment, then I understood. My
place as guide had brought me into
view, and one of those skirmishers had
tried to pick me off but had each time
made a little too much allowance for
my running.

When we neared the face of the hill
against which our charge was directed
the storm of fire first went harmlessly
over our heads, then it ceased; and
stumbling through a thicket of brush
and felled trees, we came suddenly
upon a great, frowning earthwork.
How its yellow sides loomed up!

And just over its edge the muzzles of two great brass guns gaped at us ; but everything within was silent as death. The same thought flashed through every mind. " They are lying low for us, and presently we shall look into the barrels of a row of rifles and receive their deadly volley at this short range ! " For an instant the regiment as one man recoiled and faltered. Then a serjeant from one of the centre companies stepped forth. I can see him now, a handsome, fair-haired young fellow. With cool and quiet voice he called, " Boys, let's see what's inside of this thing ! " and straight up the slope of the yellow mound he started and the regiment followed with a cheer. We found a deserted fort. It had been outflanked by the regiment on our right. They received from another side the volley which we narrowly missed and it laid low more than a hundred of their men. Away to our right, all along the line the charge had been successful and the heights of Fredericksburg were won.

Is there any intoxication like the joy of victory? For the moment men forget everything else: fatigue, thirst, wounds, dead and suffering comrades, the parting shots of fleeing foe. But it is a short-lived joy; at least ours was, for the victory had been costly and there were sad gaps in the ranks of all the regiments as we reformed on the crest of the hills. Moreover, our work was but begun. The Sixth Corps had been ordered to join Hooker by cutting a road for itself through Lee's army.

Regaining our knapsacks, we were speedily on the march, the First Division now in the advance, as ours, the Second, had been in the morning. Ghastly sights met us as we passed

2

through the old town where the Light
Division had charged; almost every
house showed marks of shot or shell,
and here and there on the sidewalks or
at street corners, in the hot sunshine
lay the dead bodies of poor heroes
whose last battle was fought. I remember how almost always some comrade's friendly hand had pulled the
corner of a blanket over their swollen
and blackening faces. On we went
leaving the town behind, marching
along a well-made high-road into a
country of small fields set in the midst
of dense and scrubby pine woods and
the afternoon was wearing away when
suddenly, from the direction in which
we were going, out of those mysterious
thickets of pine came the Song.

This time there was no prelude of
cracking rifles and whispering bullets;
but, as though some mighty hand smote
at once all the bass notes of a great

organ the cannonade roared out, swelling louder and louder all along our front. Soon we reached an open field where an ammunition train was parked and here we were halted to rest and replenish our cartridge boxes while the fierce roar of the Song still thundered until, as we were thus busied, there was a hush — one of those instant and ominous silences which smite the heart more loudly than any sound : the Song did not die away, it stopped. And then, after a breathless moment a new movement of the symphony began.   Like the pattering roar of rain after thunder, or like the long roll from a hundred tenor drums it swept along and swelled out until the woods responsive seemed to vibrate to its rattle.   It was the file-fire of the line of battle.   We could see nothing, not even the smoke through the dense forest; we could only listen. " Hark! " said an old soldier standing near me. " D' ye hear that? Bullets this time: Them 's the little things that kills !"

But swiftly now we are on the march again, pressing toward the sound of the Song. And soon the wounded begin to appear, making their way past us toward the rear by the side paths of the road on which we march; every moment their numbers increase until we find ourselves marching between two ghastly lines of wounded men: only a detachment from the growing company of the victims of the Song, only those who can walk. But there were gruesome sights in that procession of pain. Here a man holding up his hand across which a bullet has ploughed a bloody track; there one with a ragged hole through his cheek; then an officer leaning on two other men, both wounded, the ashy hue of death on his face and the blood streaming from his breast. This is no picture of the imagination. I am telling things that I saw, things that burned themselves into my memory; and I remember that every one of those wounded men whether his hurt were great or small, was pale as death and wore a fixed expression, not of terror but of stony despair. They all walked slowly and wearily and if you asked one of them, "How is the battle going?" you got the invariable answer, "Our regiment is all cut to pieces;" and they said it in a tone of tired reproach as though you ought to know and had insulted them by asking, or else with an inflection which meant, "Presently you will catch it yourselves." It was a procession of spectres and cold cheer it furnished for us, hurrying forward toward the ever-nearing and now frightful tones of the Song; yet I think the emotion uppermost in our minds was not precisely fear but a sort of awful curiosity: we burned to see as well as hear the dreadful mystery beyond the pines; the Song seemed to come from a deadly but luring siren whose call we must obey.

But night was now coming fast and all the ways began to darken; and just when we expected to emerge into the heart of battle, as though an invisible conductor had suddenly raised his wand, as abruptly as it began the Song ceased and there was a great silence. We had heard though we had not seen the fight at Salem Church, a bitterly contested but drawn battle in which many hundreds of brave men fell. The Sixth Corps had begun to feel the weight of Lee's army.

The night which followed was one of those sweet nights of early summer when earth seems not to sleep, but to unloosen her bands and lie down to play with her merry brood of new-born children. Yet there was strange mystery abroad : everywhere a weird sound —was it of sorrow or of foreboding, nature's wail or nature's warning? It seemed to mingle both as the May moon shone down on those who died to-day and those who were to die to-morrow. I have often heard the spirit-like cry of the whippoorwill, but never as I heard it that night. It came from every tree and bush, from every side and all around until it pervaded all the air. Perhaps I thought more of it because I was not one of the fortunate ones who could sleep undisturbed. The first serjeant was among the missing, the second serjeant had to take his duty and I was obliged to act as "commissary," rouse a detail of sleepy and unwilling men, stumble through the fields with them until we found the supply train and bring back a load of rations for the company; but I never hear a whippoorwill that I do not think of that night.

In the morning we found a little brook near our lines; it was a welcome friend; it offered us water for coffee and for a much-needed wash and its banks were speedily lined with chaffing, gossiping, half-dressed soldiers. But the coffee-pots had scarce begun to send their grateful fragrance through the lines when that monotonously awful Song broke forth again. From the hills in our rear which we had victoriously assaulted yesterday, came screaming shells from an enemy's battery. Our breakfast was cut short: "Fall in, men!" "Attention, battalion!" The orders flew from rank to rank, and soon the lines were formed. A pleasant Virginia mansion stood on rising ground near by, and the pretty lawn in front offered a good position which was speedily taken by one of our batteries, the horses ruthlessly trampling down the flowers and shrubbery; and there before that peaceful home the war-dogs began their baying answer to the hostile shots. Meantime the regiments were in motion and as we crossed a field below the house its fleeing occupants went by us. I was near enough to see them closely: an intelligent-looking man with his fair, pale wife and two little children. They were friends of our foes, but every heart ached for them and we let them pass in respectful silence. I noticed that the man's face bore the same set, despairing expression that I had seen the day before in the faces of the wounded men. A new and horrid discord sounded in the Song as that sad little company went by.

The firing soon ceased; but all the morning we marched and counter-marched taking up first one, then another position, while now and then in the valleys below we caught glimpses of the brown ranks of the Confederates who seemed pouring in from all sides. The situation was evident even to us in the ranks.   Hooker had abandoned the Sixth Corps and Lee was concentrating all his available force to crush us. Things looked desperate.   I remember that Joe tried all day to keep the bearings of the river in mind, and proposed that, if worst came to worst we should, even under fire attempt to swim it rather than go to Andersonville.

But the day passed quietly, all the afternoon we lay in a little field with woods on three sides, in apparent security and the men talked and joked and laughed as though battles were a far-off story.   Thus time wore on, until toward evening a distant cannon shot sounded; then another, and a spent shell came harmlessly over the tree-tops tumbling end over end to the ground; and then, all at once, pandemonium seemed let loose. It was the Song in another of its wild and wonderful variations. As yesterday at Salem Church there was no prelude of skirmish fire; but unlike yesterday's evening Song, this did not begin with the growl of the bulldogs. All instruments of wrath and war seemed taking part in it, and it came, not from our front alone but from the right, from the left, from the woods before us; while out in the open space a battery of ours was savagely firing at an enemy we could not see. Quickly but quietly we formed in line. Even now I can see my dear comrade, Serjeant W——, passing along the company front counting off the files in his grave, careful way. Then he took his place next the captain, and I saw him no more: he fell in the battle, a noble young Christian, with a wife and child waiting for him in the faraway home to which he never returned.

Presently our orders came, and we moved at double-quick past the wood out into a larger field which sloped gently toward a dry ditch and then rose in the same manner on the farther side. Coming over the opposite crest of the slope, in full view was a brigade of the enemy; another body of them was well up into the wood in front of the field we were leaving; beside us now was our battery already mentioned: we could hear the captain shouting his orders for the timing of the shells in seconds and half-seconds. It was getting too hot for him: his horses were beginning to fall and to save his guns he was, as we passed him, calling out to his men to "limber up and be off."

Every incident of that scene is wonderfully vivid to me even to-day. I was conscious of none of "the frenzy of battle," but, instead, every sense seemed more than naturally quickened. I remember that, as we entered the larger field and the panorama of war opened full before me and the Song roared its diapason I thought and said to myself, "How inexpressibly grand this is!" And I noticed everything: the very colour of the ground and of the evening light and the brown ranks of the oncoming foe; and a little tragedy that was being enacted at one side, which I always think of as illustrative of the sort of stuff which was to be found in that old Army of the Potomac and of the grit which makes the Anglo-Saxon the hardest of all men to conquer. A small regiment of veterans, either a Maine or a Wisconsin regiment — I never certainly knew which — was in that field, and as we came near they were being outflanked by the enemy

who were penetrating the woods at
close range. Their position was un-
tenable, they were suffering severely
and the regulation move for them
would have been to fall back; but
instead they deliberately changed front
and moved up nearer, wheeling slowly
by battalion, not an easy manœuvre
even on the parade ground; and they
did it without ceasing or even slacken-
ing their fire; and all the while they
had to close up the gaps left in their
ranks by men who were dropping,
dropping, dropping, to the savage fire
of the foe.

I suppose the commander of the
division thought such raw troops as
we, fit only for sacrifice. At any rate,
we were rushed to the bottom of the
field and posted in the ditch to check
the onset of a Confederate brigade as
best we might. It is needless to say
that we suffered severely, or that we

could hold our desperate position only for a little while. But our fire must have told, for the enemy swerved to the right as we opened on them; yet they kept coming on and soon began to outflank us.

The same strange intensity of perception with which I entered the field stayed with me and photographed its scenes upon my mind. I can see the man several files away, just too far for me to reach, who vexed me because in his excitement he would, every time he fired shoot before he aimed with his rifle pointed toward the sky; and little S——, a boy whom we were all fond of, shot through the body yet coolly walking off toward the rear saying, "Well, boys, I'm hit!" And I can hear our brave but eccentric lieutenant-colonel shouting: "Give it to them! Give them Blissom!" And I remember that just above my head there seemed to be a stratum of flying bullets so that in loading, every time I was about to raise my arm to ram down the charge I said to myself, " Here goes a bullet through this arm." And yet, at the same time I noticed the vicious snips with which the grass-blades all about were being cut. How any one escapes in close battle is a mystery; yet the killed and wounded are almost always a small minority.

Strange to say, the companies on the left, which were most exposed held out longest and when, as was inevitable the regiment broke, many of their men and officers refused to run but retired fighting stubbornly. I remember how one captain, a fiery little man tried to hold his men together, how he implored and threatened and swore at them and drew his revolver upon them and at last, when it was no use flung himself down upon the ground and cried like a baby;

and how another, a tall German whose company was next to ours held his men to their work nobly until they could be held no longer, and then with slow and moody steps walked up that deadly slope muttering oaths to himself and switching off the grass-blades with his sword. Some veterans who saw him told me afterward that they expected every moment to see him drop.

Our regiment was not the only broken one: the whole front line was apparently gone; the sudden savage charge of twice our number was sweeping everything before it. As the fragments of our company retired up the slope of the field, a few, of whom I happened to be one came to a slightly sunken road, a mere farm track, but in it lay the Sixth Regiment of the old Vermont Brigade. As they saw us they called out, " Rally on us, boys !" and we gladly accepted the invitation. Several weeks before I had been on duty on the picket line : it was the reserve and we were allowed to kindle fires, and all night by the blazing logs I had talked to a young Vermonter, a plain Green Mountain farmer lad, and we had made a soldier's friendship. When I came to the sunken road the first man I saw in that prone line of men was my camp-fire friend. I called out to him and dropped by his side. Others of our men did likewise and we lengthened out their too short line by about a dozen files.

It was apparently the last desperate hope of the corps. Our division commander, sitting on his horse and watching us is reported to have said to one of his aides, " If that line breaks, we're gone ! "

We lay at full length on the ground, silent save for the exhortation of the

officers : " Hold your fire, boys ! "
" Keep quiet, there ! " " Down with
that rifle ! " For we had reached the
point where heed of consequences was
gone and a cold recklessness had taken
possession of us and it was hard to
restrain the men.

On came the Confederates, their
" rebel yell " now sounding shrill and
clear ; and they were firing as they
came with so deadly an aim that
several of our officers who rose up
slightly the better to control their
men were hit and fell back dead or
wounded.

They crossed the ditch where our
regiment had been and we could see
each separate star and bar upon their
red battle-flags and their slouch hats
pulled down to shield their eyes from
the setting sun, and then their very
faces. I remember how I singled out
one after another and admired certain big

brown beards as they swarmed up the slope straight toward us.

They were almost on us — some of the men said, not ten feet away, but perhaps imagination shortened the distance — when the Vermont colonel, who, as I remember wore a long, black rubber coat over his uniform and looked like a Methodist parson shouted out the command: " Rise! Fire!"

Like spectres looming from the grave, the line of men stood up, and the Song shrieked out in one awful death-laden volley. The field before us was changed as though by some dire magic. A moment before it had been filled with a yelling, charging host; now it was suddenly cleared. As though an October gust had swept across that May evening, away down to the bottom of the field and beyond the ground was strewn with brown, prostrate forms; but they were not leaves, they were dead and wounded men!

The little Vermont regiment had repulsed and shattered a charging Louisiana brigade. We followed up our volley with a counter-charge, our own regiment meanwhile had rallied and joined us, and when we came to the ditch where we had at first been posted dead men lay across and within it, and from their midst living men who had sought refuge from our fire arose, waving their hands in token of surrender: among these the colonel commanding the Confederate brigade.

As he stood up a big, impetuous Scotch-Irishman confronted him with his bayonet, and the savage exclamation:

" Give me yer soord or I'll r-run ye through!"

The colonel was a stately Southern gentleman whose soldierly spirit was unbroken by misfortune.

"No!" he sternly replied, looking disdainfully at the levelled steel. "I yield my sword to no private. Show me a commissioned officer!"

It is hard to say how it might have ended, for Hodge was a dour man; but our lieutenant-colonel was fortunately close at hand. He ordered the soldier away and received the officer's surrender in a manner worthy of them both.

The setting sun was throwing its parting gleams across that awful little field, the Song had sobbed itself into silence, the Sixth Corps was saved, and night's curtain fell upon the last scene in the drama of Chancellorsville.

The
Making of a Regiment

THE process by which men were made soldiers in our late war was one of the most remarkable things in that phenomenal conflict. Men who had no taste for military life, no desire for martial glory, and none save the most rudimentary military training were enlisted, uniformed, organised into regiments, officered often with those as ignorant of war as themselves, equipped, armed, and sent into the field within a few months, or even a few weeks, after being mustered into service. And these raw regiments were speedily moulded into well-disciplined and effective battalions, fit to be members of a famous army.

All this is history more or less well known, but the way in which the result was accomplished is not so familiar, and perhaps the experience of one who was a member of one of these regiments may be worth telling.

I remember — I was but a boy then — how, at the time of the news from Sumter and the President's first call for troops, the pastor of the village church spoke on a Sunday morning to a breath-less congregation and closed with the trumpet call, "Who will go to the war?"

Instantly in the gallery one man stood up. He was a veteran who had served in the regular army in Mexico. There were others, but I mention him because he was typical. Into the ear-liest formed regiments went the few like the soldier of Mexico who had seen actual warfare, also the pick of the members of the city militia organisations; and into these first regiments went the enthusiasm of the nation's first burst of patriotism. Then, too, the delays of the first year of the war gave opportunity for drill and discipline of the regulation sort, often under officers of West Point training. These oldest regiments were, therefore, the flower of the army, and in a peculiar way the model and foundation of it. But after Gettysburg — indeed, before that memorable battle — they had become terribly reduced in number, and actually formed but a fraction of the mighty host.

The history of the later regiments was different. Enthusiasm, though it did not die, cooled. Something else took its place, something more truly characteristic of the great crisis. I do not know how to give it a name. It

was a spirit that entered into the
nation, a solemn and compelling impulse that seized upon men whether
they would or no.   Many attempted
to resist, but successful resistance was
blasting to peace of mind.   The voice
of this spirit asked insistently, " Why
do you not go to the war ? "   And
it was not easy for an able-bodied man
to prove his right to stay at home.   It
was in obedience to this impulse that
men went into regiments formed during
the year of 1862.   The day for illusions
was passing ; the grim character of the
struggle was becoming too evident.
" Going to the war " meant no possibility of holiday excursion, for the stress
of the crisis hastened new regiments to
the front with small delay ; the calls for
troops were urgent, and they summoned
to serious work.   It was by one of these
calls that we were mustered, and it was
marvellous how quickly ten full compa-

nies were enlisted in the county. Local
pride had its influence ; the county
contained one large manufacturing town
and several important villages. Town
vied with country, and each village with
every other, in completing its quota of
men. There were other influences.
"A draft" was beginning to be talked
of, and there were some who said, " I
would rather volunteer now than be
drafted a few months later." Then,
too, for the first time, a bounty was
promised. It was small in comparison
with the sums afterwards offered, but
sufficient to turn the scale with waverers.
And yet the chief impulse was that imperious spirit of the hour which had
begotten the feeling in every man's
breast that until he had offered himself
to his country he owed an unpaid debt;
and when a regiment was actually in
process of organisation in your own
neighbourhood, this was brought home

with redoubled force; when friends and neighbours to whom perhaps the sacrifice was greater than it possibly could be to yourself came forward, very shame made it difficult to hold back. Men really too old for service forgot a few years of their life and persuaded the mustering officer to wink at the deception. Boys, whose too glaring minority had alone prevented them thus far, yet in whose ardent hearts the spirit of the hour burned the more hotly by delay, sprang to the opportunity. In our own company there were a few men over forty-five years of age, and a much larger number of whom it would be a stretch of truth to say they were eighteen. It was pretty much the same throughout the ten companies. There were labouring men and mechanics, manufacturers and their employees, storekeepers and clerks, a few farmers, and a few students. There were young men from the best families in the county and some ne'er-do-wells, but the mass of the company and of the regiment was composed of plain, intelligent men, workers in the industries of a busy community. As to nationality, there were a few Germans and a sprinkling of Irish, but the body of the regiment was American of old and solid New England and Dutch stock.

We enlisted on a strictly equal footing, and chose our own company officers. The field officers, the colonel, lieutenant-colonel, and major, were elected by the company officers and appointed by the governor of the State. The non-commissioned officers, the serjeants and corporals, were selected by the captains.

The captain of our own company was a jeweller and an old member of a city militia organisation. Our first lieutenant was a banker's clerk, and our second lieutenant a mechanic who had in some way acquired an excellent knowledge of tactics. These were fair examples of the officers of the regiment. Out of the forty or more of them, ten had served in the State militia; a few of these ten had been with the "three months' men" who were called out at the beginning of the war; scarcely one of them had ever seen a shot fired in anger; the large majority, like the mass of the men, were destitute of any real military knowledge.

As to the colonelcy, the officers had fixed their desires upon a member of one of the old regiments, a highly qualified man; but the State authorities, in their inscrutable wisdom refused to appoint him, and sent us instead a staff officer who, though he had seen some slight service, was ignorant of infantry tactics and without experience in actual command. He was, however, an imposing individual, a fine horseman, with a decidedly military bearing and a self-assurance which temporarily concealed his defects.

Such, then, was the regiment when it was ready to be mustered into the service. You might say, " This is not a regiment ; it is a mob," and you would be wrong. The men had gone through no such process of drill as is considered essential to the making of soldiers, yet they were not utterly ignorant even in this matter. It would have been hard at that time to find a young American who did not know something of the rudiments of infantry tactics. The political campaigns immediately preceding the war, with their semi-military organisations and their nightly processions, were a preparation for what followed which has been too little noticed. And when the war began, in every village " Home Guards " or drill classes were formed, and Hardee's and Casey's " Tactics " were well known and carefully studied books. We were all inexperienced, but only a small minority of the thousand men and officers were absolutely ignorant of military drill; moreover the mass of them were intelligent Americans, who learned quickly and easily. When we left the home camp a few weeks after enrolment, we could march deceptively well, and the regiment actually received praise for its fine appearance from spectators whose frequent opportunities had made them critical. Yet we were sadly defective. To keep step, to march by companies, to execute self-consciously a few motions of the manual of arms, is but the alphabet of tactics. The battalion, not the company is the tactical unit, and until a regiment has mastered the battalion drill and has learned skirmish work, it is unfit for modern warfare. In these essential things we were utterly unpractised.

There is also something else more important than drill. With regularly trained troops perfection of drill is simply the index of discipline. We were, in fact, very imperfect in both. Our discipline was certainly lax, yet even this was not wholly lacking. We were not a crowd of enthusiasts. Even at home we had for a year and a half lived in an atmosphere of war ; the breath of battle from afar had reached us ; we knew something of what it meant to be soldiers and what we were going into. The spirit of the hour enveloped us, and when we were formally mustered in and, with our right hands raised to heaven, took the oath of service, there was no wild cheering ; there was instead a feeling of awe. The soul of the army, the mysterious solidarity of the mighty compelling organisation, seemed to take possession of us ; we knew that we

4

were no longer our own.   Discipline
is already half learned when men are
thus made ready for it.

Washington was our first destination.
We made the journey in freight cars,
and on our arrival went into camp
under canvas for the first time.   It was
shortly after the battle of Antietam,
and the city was half camp, half
hospital.   Everywhere one met the
monotonous blue uniforms : officers
hurrying hither and thither ; wounded
convalescents, pale and weary, stroll-
ing about ; sentries and squads of
provost guards ; occasionally a brigade
of dusty and tattered veterans from the
front, marching through the streets ;
and near the railroad stations, train-
loads of wounded men who had been
brought in from the overcrowded field
hospitals, lying on the floors of box
cars, the stench of their undressed
hurts filling the air.   Everywhere the

atmosphere of war emptied of its glamour !

The Capital was the sore heart of the nation, and our glimpse of it was a wholesome lesson. It sobered us; it took away all lingering sense of insubordination, and taught us the relentless power of the mighty machine of which we had become a part, and into which we knew we must be fitted.

In a few days we were sent to Frederick City, and our army life began in earnest. For more than a week we slept without tents, upon the ground, under the open sky. We also took final leave of railroad transportation. We had to learn the use of our feet and the meaning of the march. After a short stay at Frederick, orders came to proceed to Hagerstown. Western Maryland was at that time strongly held by the Union forces, yet it was not a perfectly secure country. It was subject to raids of the enemy's cavalry, and there was a spice of danger in our march.   We proceeded by easy stages ; though, unseasoned as we were, the ten or twelve miles a day with our heavy loads seemed long enough ; and at night when we made our bivouac we took carefully guarded positions and threw out pickets.   Once there was a rumour that Stewart's raiders were in the   neighbourhood, and   our   colonel made us a little speech in his bravado style.   He told us that we must not load   our   muskets, " that   he   greatly preferred the bayonet ! "   Fortunately, we   were   unmolested.   Everywhere along our march through that beautiful Maryland hill country we saw the marks of war.   We crossed the famous South Mountain and a corner of the Antietam   battlefield.   There   were groups of lonely graves by the roadside, and here and there the white tents of lingering field hospitals. On one night we camped near Phil. Kearney's old brigade, one regiment of which had come from our own neighbourhood. Some of us went over to their camp to visit friends whom we had not seen since the beginning of the war. We saw the evening dress parade of that choice regiment. They were fresh from the perils and hardships of the campaign; their ranks were sadly thinned, their clothes worn to rags, many of the men were nearly shoeless; but their rifles and their fighting equipments were in perfect order, and their dress parade was performed with a precision which could scarcely have been surpassed had they been a battalion of regulars in garrison with spotless uniforms and white gloves.

When we reached Hagerstown we found that we were assigned to a brigade of veterans, Yankees from the far

North, who had come from their ancestral mountain farms at the first call of their country. They were, in many respects, a contrast to our friends whose dress parade we had witnessed. For those military forms and ceremonies so dear to the heart of the professional soldier they had small regard. They were noted foragers. Their commander, an officer of the regular army who afterwards became a distinguished division chief, said of them with mingled vexation and admiration, " I never saw such men. It is impossible to tire them out. No matter how far or how hard you march them, at night they will be all over the country stealing pigs and chickens." Their five regiments were all from one State, and their *esprit de corps* was very strong. With quaint Yankee drawl they used to boast, " This old brigade has never been broke, and it never shall be."

And I think they made good their word to the end. They obeyed their officers with prompt devotion, but only because they knew that this was a necessary part of discipline; they had small reverence for rank or place. One of them once said to me, "When I am on guard, if I see an officer coming I always try to be at the other end of my beat, so that I won't have to salute him." And yet in small essentials these men were very precise soldiers. One evening one of them came over from his regiment to visit us. The enemy suddenly opened fire from his batteries away beyond the river. It was a common occurrence. There was no special danger; the regiments were not even formed in line; yet this veteran promptly took his leave. "You know," he said, "that when firing begins a man ought to be in his place in his own company." It was so always. With all their independence and contempt for conventionalities, the discipline prevailing in that brigade was really most rigid. They were not fond of reviews, and took no special pains to make a show on such occasions; but to see the splendid line they kept in that deadly charge on the Fredericksburg heights, when one of their small regiments lost over a hundred men in a few moments, was enough to bring tears of admiration from a soldier's eyes; and at Salem Heights, when at evening Stonewall Jackson's men, concentrated in overwhelming force, came down upon us in sudden, savage charge, and the brigade at our right was "smashed like a pitcher thrown against a rock," when every other hope seemed gone, these Yankees stood firm, with unbroken ranks, and saved the Sixth Corps from disaster.

These were the soldiers whose example became our chief teacher in the art of war. Greenhorns as we were, they received us kindly into their fellowship, and, while they criticised freely, they were ever ready to give us full meed of praise for anything we did well.

We were scarcely settled in our brigade camp before orders came which set the whole army in motion. From picturesque Hagerstown we marched toward the Potomac, and encamped for a few days in a grove of magnificent oaks. There was some musical talent of the popular sort in our regiment, and it had crystallised into a glee club whose free concerts about the camp-fires were the delight of the whole brigade and did much to make us pleasantly acquainted with our new friends. One of the men was an expert performer on the banjo, and he had brought his dearly beloved instrument with him. Poor fellow, he was more fit for the concert-room than for a soldier's life, and a few weeks afterward he succumbed to the toil of the march. He " straggled " and was gobbled, banjo and all, by the Confederate cavalry, and we saw him no more.

Reluctantly we left our pleasant camp under the oaks, and a short march brought us to the banks of the Potomac and in view of a pontoon bridge. That river was a Rubicon. On the other side of it lay the debatable land, the region of bloody battle, and the bridge which, like a dark line of fate lay across the water in the glow of twilight, seemed the final decision of our destiny. We had dreamed that we were to be employed in garrison duty to relieve older and more experienced troops. Now we knew that we must take our share, raw as we were, in the toil and peril of the coming campaign. Soldiers never know their destination on the march. Even the officers, unless they be corps or division commanders, are usually as much in the dark as the humblest privates, and the river, with its pontoon bridge was a revelation to our veteran friends as well as to ourselves. We listened to their comments with hushed attention. " Well, here we are once more ; here is the river and there are the pontoons, and we are going over into Virginia again. The inhabitants of the land are all rebels, and yet the last time we were over there our generals were mighty tender toward them. No foraging was allowed, and we submitted tamely ; we spared the inhabitants. But this time, may the gods do so to us and more also if we spare them ! "

There was something of the Cromwellian spirit among these Yankees, and in spite of the provost guard, they made good their threat.

The crossing of that river in the morning marked a new stage in the making of the regiment. We entered upon our first real discipline, and it was that of the march. Our tramp through Maryland, which had seemed so severe, was really child's play. Now we were part of a great campaigning host, a mere unit in the moving mass in which we must perforce keep our place. The discipline of the march may seem very simple, and it is in fact, simpler in some ways than people suppose who have formed their ideas from what they have seen in city parades. The tactics of the march are elementary. The soldier must know how to keep his place in a column of fours ; the regiment must be able instantly to form in line. That is about all. On the march there is no attempt at keeping step; there is far less apparent order than in a political parade. Each man carries his gun as he pleases, only so that he interferes with no one else. Yet, with loose order and apparent freedom there is really severest restraint. The ranks must be kept closed up; to lag, even when you are most weary is a fault; to drop out of your place and "straggle" is a crime. A man is but a cog in the wheels of a remorseless machine, and he must move with it. The march is an art which some otherwise well-drilled troops are slow in acquiring. A regiment of infantry is seldom allowed the road. When an army is moving through a hostile country, the roads are monopolised by the artillery and the supply and ammunition trains; foot soldiers must take to the fields, find a way over ploughed ground or meadow, through fences, through brush, through woods, across bridgeless streams. In spite of obstacles the column must press on keeping its formation intact, and keep closed up. This is no simple matter.

Battle is one trial of a soldier's quality; the march is another scarcely less severe. It tries endurance. Did you ever walk twenty miles in a day? It is not a long walk, and it may be delightful. But if you have had to carry even a light satchel or a fish-basket with your wading-boots, you know how the trifling load tells before the day is over; how you try it first in one position, then in another, and each seems worse than the last. Now suppose yourself loaded with knapsack containing your half of a shelter tent, your blanket, and a few other necessaries; haversack filled with three days' rations; cartridge-box with from forty to sixty rounds of ammunition; canteen

of water, heavy musket and bayonet —
fifty or sixty pounds in all.   Your
twenty miles will equal forty without
the load ; yes, more than that, even if
you could walk at will and choose the
easiest paths, which is precisely what
the soldier cannot do.   You must
stumble over stony places, and push
through briers, and wallow through
swampy ground, or toil through soft
fields ; now and then you must wade a
brook up to your knees or deeper, and
for the next hour your shoes will weigh
a pound more than they ought and
gather mud and absorb gravel.   Perhaps the regiment may take the high-
road for a time, and the dust, beaten
small and deep by preceding hoofs and
wheels will enshroud you in a horrible
cloud from which there is no escape, and
penetrate every crevice of your clothing,
and fill your eyes and ears and mouth
and nostrils, and blind and choke you.

There is no martial music to cheer
you on; only the monotonous command, "Close up, men!" You lose
consciousness of your soul, you know
only that you have a body. Even that
seems not to belong to you, it seems a
badly oiled machine, part of a greater
machine. And, then, on hot days the
thirst! Your canteen will soon be ex-
hausted; you will look with longing
eyes at every stagnant puddle, and
when a brook is reached — I have then
seen men break through all restraint
and madly dash at the water in spite
of the drawn swords of officers vainly
struggling to keep the ranks whole.
As the day wanes the weariness amounts
to agony. Every bone aches, every
nerve is unstrung; strong men lose
their self-control, sometimes almost
their manhood.

The moods of men on the march are
a curious study. Perhaps early in the

day the whole line will break into song, especially if the route happens to be through an inhabited town. The Maryland villages used to ring with

"John Brown's body lies a-mouldering in the
  grave,
But his soul goes marching on."

Then silence will fall on every one as the burden begins to tell. Not a word will be spoken until some one breaks out with an oath, and then, all up and down the line, every man who ever swears will answer and the air will be blue with blasphemy.

War takes no account of Sabbaths. We often marched day after day until we fairly lost track of time and you might hear a dialogue like the following:

" Bill, what day is this ? "

"Why, don't you know? This is Sunday."

" By George! is that so? Well, there's no rest for the wicked!"

5

And then the men would begin to talk about home, and somehow over the rudeness of war and the weariness of the march a breath of hallowed air would seem to waft itself, and the far-off sound of Sabbath bells would seem to steal, and the dim faces of distant loved ones would rise before us, until the spell would perhaps be broken by another chorus of profanity.

By force of stern necessity we became a good marching regiment long before we had half learned tactical drill, and the discipline did several important things for us. Our marching was not peaceful; it was through a hostile country. The enemy's cavalry hung about our flanks and rear and the sound of cannon was frequent. We had as yet no fighting but we were constantly threatened, and that helped the discipline. It taught us unceasing vigilance and the need of perpetual readiness; it also tried the nerves of our officers. The unfit ones began to drop off. First our lieutenant-colonel, then our major was smitten with what the men called "cannon fever." Their health failed suddenly, their resignations were offered and accepted and we were well rid of them. The captain of Company A, who now became major, was a fine type of the class of men by whom our volunteer army was mainly officered. He was a plain citizen who had been superintendent in a manufactory, and his military knowledge was only such as could be gained in a militia company. He had however, a strong soldierly instinct, and better still, his personal character compelled respect. Familiar in manner with no "airs," yet always dignified and firm; modest, yet as we found when the test came, unflinchingly brave; with keen natural intelligence, quick to grasp a situation and prompt in action he proved that good officers are born, not made. His awkwardness on horseback afforded amusement only for a little while. In a few weeks he rode like a cavalryman, and every fresh trial of his quality raised him in our esteem and affection.

The weeding process worked among the men in a different way. The old and weak and physically unfit broke down. Some of them died; a number of them were discharged from the service. At the end of a month we had lost more officers and as many men as a smartly-contested battle would have cost us, and instead of being weaker we were distinctly stronger for it. The law of the survival of the fittest was beginning to work. In another way the weeding process proceeded. Every army requires a great many non-combatants as its servants. There must be waggoners, clerks at headquarters, ambulance drivers, hospital attendants, "detailed men" of many sorts, and each regiment has to furnish its quota of these. When, therefore, an order would come to detail a man, perhaps for ambulance driver, the colonel would send it down to a captain with the hint, "Detail the worst dead beat in your company." Sometimes these non-combatant positions were sought by those who had no stomach for the fight, and thus, in different ways, our thinned ranks became cleaner.

We learned other things by the discipline of the march. We learned to live as soldiers must. Life in a well-ordered camp and camp life in the field are vastly different. The army lived in shelter tents. These were simply pieces of cotton cloth about six feet square, and each man carried one piece on his knapsack. Two or three buttoned together and stretched over such poles or sticks as could be found, or over muskets set in the ground when nothing else could be had, formed our habitation. We literally carried our houses on our backs. We slept on the ground, or rather, we learned not to sleep on the ground. Pine branches made a luxurious bed, but anything served — dried grass, boughs of saplings, even corn stalks, though they were worse than boarding-house mattresses. I have slept on unthreshed wheat — anything to keep the body from direct contact with the ground, which, even in summer chills one through before morning. Then, wood for fires must be had. Through the hill country of Virginia we used the fences. When the welcome halt was called at evening and arms stacked, it was a sight to see eight or nine hundred men joining with wild cheers in a mad charge on the nearest rail

fence.   Sometimes our colonel would
draw us up in line and give the word,
so that all might have an even chance,
and then, after a brisk scrimmage the
fence would disappear as if by magic.
Dry rails made the best of camp-fires,
but the skill which men developed at
fire-making was wonderful.   We had
few axes beside the dozen carried by
the pioneer corps, whose duty it was
to clear obstructions from the road;
we had to break up our rails or break
down branches as best we could.   Our
jack-knives did yeoman service.   Often
green wood alone was available; and
I have actually seen fires kindled in
the midst of pouring rain with nothing
but such apparently impossible materials as green pine saplings.

Two men from each company were
detailed as cooks.   They were seldom
favourites with the men.   On the march,
and, finally, almost altogether their

services were dispensed with. We preferred to do our own cooking, especially when it came to the coffee. Coffee was our chief comfort and our main necessity. We carried it in the haversack, in a little bag with a partition : on one side ground coffee, on the other, the smaller side, a little brown sugar ; and we made it generously and drank it strong. Coffee, hardtack, and salt pork were the standard marching rations.

It was curious to notice how men treated the rations question. Three days' supply at a time was dealt out to us. Some of the men would make way with their stock in two days, and then go begging among their comrades. Upon others excessive weariness acted as a stay upon appetite, and the three days' rations would be more than enough. I think these were the men who stood the hardship of the march best.   After supper came sleep, the sleep of exhaustion; and then, at daybreak, the reveille, roll-call, hasty breakfast (like the supper, of hardtack, pork, and coffee).   Then canteens were filled from the nearest available water, knapsacks packed, and precisely at sunrise the column would be formed and the march begun.   The rule was, march two hours, rest ten minutes; except at noon, when twenty minutes' rest was allowed.

At these rests the men would lie down wherever they happened to be, and think the hard ground blessed and the time too short.   Sometimes, though this was later, during the battle season we had night marches, and as illustrating the result of the discipline of the march even upon new troops, I have seen men, when halt was called at night, lie down in the dusty road and fall instantly fast asleep;

but at the low-spoken order, " Fall in, men!" they would as instantly rise, and, before they were fully awake step into their proper places in the line. Under the discipline of the march, in three months' time we had learned lessons which the best-trained city militia regiments never learn and which made us veterans in comparison with them.

If you ask how we learned, I can only answer that we did as we saw the old troops about us doing. And it is but justice to our colonel to say that he knew the duties of the march, and especially those of the camp, and was strict to the point of severity, with the officers especially.

An army of a hundred thousand men on the march would be a wonderful sight if one could see it, but the columns stretch too far to be visible all at once. They reach for miles, and

woods or hills or valleys hide them.
But occasionally we had impressive
views from some height into the country below, over which the endless lines
moved like vast serpents, and sometimes we had curious surprises. I remember how one day our regiment
took an unfrequented road and we
seemed to be alone. No other troops
were in sight, and all day long we spec-
ulated upon our destination. Some
thought we were being sent back to
Washington for garrison duty; others
that we were detached for some special,
perhaps perilous, service. There were
all sorts of surmises, but finally night
came, and we camped on the hillside of
a long and deep valley. We lighted
our fires, and, in apparent response
other fires began to twinkle from the
hills beyond and beside us and from
down in the valley, and, as it grew
darker the fires increased in numbers

and in brightness until, in every direction, as far as the eye could see, the lonely woods seemed changed as if by magic into a vast city.   We were in the very midst of the great army; we had been marching with it all day.

Our first battle was that of Fredericksburg, and we went into it under every disadvantage.   Our showy colonel was absent on sick-leave, our only field officer was our yet untried major; in fact, not a single one of our officers had ever been really under fire and, beside our imperfection in drill, we were wretchedly armed.   In the haste to put us into the field we had been supplied with Harper's Ferry smooth-bore muskets, — antiquated weapons utterly unfit for modern warfare.   We knew they were useless except at short range; we suspected that some of them would prove more dangerous to ourselves than to the enemy.   The men despised them, and called them " stuffed clubs ; " but they saved us from being sacrificed.

I was never prouder of my regiment than at the moment when we were ordered to the front. We had been for hours exposed to a long-range artillery fire, and one regiment after another of the brigade had been sent forward until we were left alone. We knew the helplessness of our inexperience and the uselessness of our old guns ; yet when the command came there was no faltering. The men marched away with cheerful readiness, and in better line than we could often show on parade. But ere we reached the battle's bloody edge we were ordered back again. The commander of the brigade protested. He said that, armed and officered as we were, it would be sheer murder to send us in.

And so it happened that we saw that

awful battle from afar, though for two days we endured one of the most trying of the ordeals which come to soldiers. We had to lie still and be shot at. Few indeed are hit by long-range artillery fire, but every catastrophe seems doubly dreadful because you see it all and can do nothing but wonder if it will be your turn next. You fall into a dolefully speculative mood and into watching for the sound of the howling shells. You can tell if one is coming your way, but never just how near. Sometimes a shot will strike close in front and cover you with a shower of gravel, or a shell will explode over your head and rend the air with demoniac shrieks of flying fragments. Death seems even nearer and more horrible than in close battle where you can do as well as suffer.

The panorama of that battle was a never-to-be-forgotten sight. From the amphitheatre of hills on either side the river a hundred cannon roared. The space between seemed filled with a chorus of demons. In the lulls of this pandemonium, for miles along the line, the mournful, far-away skirmish fire echoed constantly, and ever and anon on that tragic Saturday, away at our right we could hear the shouts of charging men coming like a fateful wail across the field, and then the steady roll of the Confederate file fire from the deadly stone wall against which fourteen brigades were successively and vainly hurled. And every charging shout meant that men for duty's sake, but hopelessly, were meeting death by hundreds.

Incidents of that battle will always dwell in my memory. There I saw a soldier's death for the first time. We were in line with other troops well up toward the front. Beyond, in the open fields the skirmishers were at work.

We could see little of them save the puffs of smoke from their rifles. A man came over from a neighbouring regiment to speak to a friend near me. As he stood talking, a bullet from the skirmish line struck him in the breast and he fell at our feet. I can feel the shock that went through me even now.

Tragedy is scarcely ever without its by-play of comedy. We were for a time lying at rest behind a low, bare ridge which slightly protected us from the enemy's fire. Suddenly a rabbit started up from a little clump of bushes. Three or four soldiers instantly sprang after him. Presently the rabbit neared the ridge and ran to the top of it but his pursuers, now in full chase forgot all danger and followed. And the picture in my mind is that of the rabbit and his reckless hunters darkly silhouetted upon the summit of the ridge and punctuated here and there with the sudden white cloud of a bursting shell. I think the rabbit escaped; the men, I know came off unharmed.

We had had no breakfast, and when the enemy's fire lulled several of the men tried to do a little cooking. A comrade near me was busily engaged in frying a piece of pork in a pan extemporised from an old canteen. Suddenly the batteries reopened; several stacks of muskets were struck, with the effect of making them look like a nest of snakes. Our commander said, " Some of you men might as well move up nearer the ridge where there is better protection." I could see that my friend of the frying-pan was growing anxious. He looked at his pork and then at the shelter. It was hard to abandon his breakfast; but life was growing dearer every moment, and with sudden impulse he left all and ran for refuge. How

6

big Corporal J——, lying near me, laughed as he rescued and appropriated the burning pork! The man did not hear the last of that frying-pan incident for months; yet he was a brave fellow, and afterwards did his duty nobly in the face of far greater danger than any we saw that day.

Men will do queer things in battle. I knew of a regiment sent to support a battery when the enemy was about to charge. The men went to their post at the double quick with fixed bayonets, and just in front of the battery they were ordered to lie down so that the guns might fire over their heads. As they did so one man accidentally pricked another with his bayonet and the fellow, enraged, struck at him. They dared not stand up to fight for fear of having their heads blown off by the battery close behind and therefore, on their knees, under the guns they had it out in a fisticuff duel before the officers could interfere and stop them.

We lost only a few men at Fredericksburg but we gained a great experience. The battle took place in December and after it the army went into winter quarters. A field officer from one of the old regiments of the brigade was detailed to command us in the protracted absence of our colonel. He knew our defects. We needed drill. He gave it to us without stint and worked us as we had never been worked before — company and skirmish drill in the morning, battalion drill all the afternoon, so that after the evening dress parade we were as weary as bricklayers. Nothing escaped his notice; he made you feel that his eyes were on you personally and his orders came in a sharp, explosive tone that made men jump. After an hour's hard work on the drill ground, some of us would grow careless, and then that rasping voice would startle the whole battalion. "Why don't that man hold that gun *properly?*" and a half dozen muskets would straighten up with a jerk.

Under our own colonel the discipline of the regiment had been excessive in unimportant details and lax in essentials. All this was changed. We felt ourselves ruled with an iron hand, yet with just discrimination, so that while we stood in awe of our new commander we learned to like him greatly; the more so when we found that he liked us, and in a lurid, unrepeatable epigram expressed his opinion of what might have been made of us if he could have had us from the first. Then, too, he looked carefully after our comfort and our necessities. Some rascally quartermaster had nearly starved us with bad rations. He quickly stopped that.

Moreover, to our great satisfaction, new rifles for the regiment arrived. We gladly bade good-bye to our old "stuffed clubs," and we had occasional target practice with our new and effective weapons. A fresh spirit came into us; we imagined ourselves fit for anything.

Yet the regiment was really like a great boy who begins to think himself a man. The weeding process was still incomplete and progressing. Captains and lieutenants disappeared one by one. Some who were otherwise competent had broken down in health; others had been proved unfit. Their places were filled by promotions, mainly of non-commissioned officers.

Our experience was precisely that of almost every volunteer regiment in the army. After the first twelve months' service the line was usually transformed. Serjeants and corporals, men who had been appointed because of fitness rather than chosen because of popularity or influence came into command as company officers. In much less than a year not a single one of our original field officers remained, and only three of the ten original captains of companies.

As to the men in general, the weeding process showed some results worthy of record. It proved that very few men over forty years of age were fit for war, either physically or morally, and that boys from eighteen to twenty made excellent soldiers. It was not simply that the young fellows were more reckless, but they never worried about coming danger. They were more cheerful ; they fretted less over privations ; they actually endured hardships better than older and stronger men. Our losses among the boys were chiefly in battle ; our losses among the old men were mainly by sickness and physical exhaustion.   Doubtless it might be different with a body of men carefully selected and gradually inured to a soldier's life, but in our volunteer regiments, hastily enlisted and composed of men whose habit of life was suddenly changed, the facts as observed in our experience would, I think, always hold good.

The monotony of camp life was broken by frequent picket duty.   This was sometimes dangerous and often trying, especially to the non-commissioned officers on whom special responsibility rested; yet in pleasant weather at least, it was a welcome change from the dull routine of camp.   It was also an essential part of our education.   Pickets are the antennæ of an army.   In the face of the enemy the antennæ become formidable as skirmishers.   A picket line, in case of need is quickly transformed into a skirmish line.   Nothing teaches vigilance, the use of independent judgment, prompt action in emergency, and at the same time strict subordination, like outpost or skirmish work. We had some exciting and some amusing experiences.

One night the line ran through a swamp. It was moonlight, and in the small hours toward morning things looked weird and ghostly. In visiting my sentries I came to one of our boys, a mere stripling, whom I found in a state of high excitement. "Serjeant," he said, "I wish I could be relieved; I'm afraid to stay here." I asked him what the trouble was and he answered, "There's a wolf out there," pointing to a dismal clump of bushes. "I saw him come out of the woods and go across the swamp into those bushes. He was close to me. I do wish I could be relieved; I'm afraid to stay here alone!"

I knew it was a trick of the imagination, or possibly a stray fox, and told him so; but it was of no use. The poor fellow's terror was pitiful. Yet that same boy was afterward as bold as a lion when bullets were flying thick and men were falling about him.

Toward the end of January there were rumours in the air. They furnished food for camp gossip, and were beginning to leave us sceptical, when orders came suddenly, and we found ourselves one gray morning actually on the move — where or why we knew not, though it was clear that no ordinary enterprise was at hand; for the whole army was in motion, and in all our experience, never had a march been so forced. It was hurry, hurry, almost at a trot, with rests so infrequent and so short that men, from sheer inability to keep the pace began to drop out of the ranks. The roads were good, but the sky was overcast and when, early in the evening we halted and pitched our shelter tents for the night, the weather was threatening. Before morning a cold, northeast storm had set in; all day long the icy rain poured down. The Virginia roads were speedily melting into muddy creeks. The movement of artillery or pontoons was fast becoming an impossibility; but at nightfall a desperate attempt was made. Our regiment was among the unfortunates detailed to extricate the ponderous pontoon train from its muddy fetters. Imagine a bridge of boats loaded upon waggons, each great flat-bottomed boat about twenty feet long, and alternating with the boats, waggon-trucks loaded with bridge timbers, six or eight horses to each of these unwieldy vehicles, and the whole train hopelessly mired in a rough wood road; wheels sunk to the hubs, horses floundering helplessly, some of them half

dead with their terrible work ; the night
dark, the half-frozen rain pouring piti-
lessly — and then perhaps you may
picture the task which was ours.   Muskets, equipments, even overcoats were
left at our tents.   We were marched
about a mile to the place where the
pontoons were stalled ; ropes were made
fast to the waggons and, with a hundred
men to each, we dragged them one after
another out of the woods into open
ground.   There they sank more hopelessly than ever.   The force of men
had to be doubled.   We could have
drawn them far more easily without
wheels ; but at last, when it was nearly
midnight they were all ranged upon
solid ground on a little knoll.

As to ourselves, we were drenched
with the rain, bruised with our falls,
half frozen with the cold, and plastered
with mud from head to foot.   And in
this plight we were kept standing idly

for a bitter hour, waiting for another division of the pontoon train. But it never came, and finally we were permitted to return to our tents where we found everything, even our blankets soaked with the merciless rain.

The work and exposure had been horrible. I remember, as we marched back to camp seeing one poor fellow, a member of a veteran regiment, who had apparently gone crazy under the strain ; he was screaming and swearing wildly, while his comrades vainly strove to calm him.

By morning the failure of the enterprise, which was an attempt to surprise the enemy, was evident. The retreat of the army through the mud and the rain which followed was an experience the horror of which none that shared it can forget. The elements were the foes which prevailed against us then, and the demoralisation of the army was worse than any we ever saw inflicted by battle with mortals. Many men died from exposure and exhaustion. This was the famous " mud march."

Winter passed quickly after this, and with the spring came preparation for a new campaign. Our jaunty colonel had recovered his health and returned to duty ; the list of field officers was completed by the appointment of a new lieutenant-colonel. All that we knew of him was that he had served with distinction upon General Hancock's staff. He was eccentric in manner, evidently unpractised in the handling of an infantry regiment, and we took to him none too kindly at first. But when we came to know him his high character, his resourcefulness and his noble courage won our admiration and our profound respect. He was destined soon to become the commander of the regiment.

The last step, the most important of all, in the making of the regiment was now before us. At the first Fredericksburg we had endured the trial of battle partially and passively. The more real and active experience was now before us. We were members of Sedgwick's Corps, whose brilliant capture of the Fredericksburg heights turned the tide of disaster at the battle of Chancellorsville and failed to pluck victory from defeat only because of the unaccountable inertness of the commander of the Union forces. Our regiment was one of those chosen to form part of one of the storming columns. It may seem strange that new troops should be selected for such perilous and difficult duty, yet this was often done. The new regiments were strong in numbers; they had not been decimated by battle and disease; and though less reliable than older battalions, when no complicated manœuvres were required, when the only thing was to go straight forward against a fire from the front their wild *élan* sometimes accomplished wonders. They were seldom spared in close battle; it was a way, though a costly one, to break them in and make soldiers of them. The heaviest losses often fell upon them.

Placed between two other regiments of the brigade, in a sunken road where we were sheltered from the enemy's fire, we anxiously awaited the signal for the assault. We could see something of the work before us. Nearly a mile of open field lay between us and the base of the hills whose crests were crowned with the Confederate earthworks, and every foot of that open ground was swept by their fire. It must be crossed before the storming column could reach the heaviest part of its task and begin the real assault upon those deadly hills. All along at our right, away up into the

streets of Frederick a mile or more away
other columns were stationed at intervals, some of them facing stronger de-
fences than those against which our
attack was to be directed.

At noon precisely, the signal guns
boomed out and we sprang to the
charge. From the very first our colonel blundered. He failed to obey his
orders ; he led us wildly in a wrong
direction under the very guns of one
of our own batteries. The hills in front
of us flamed and roared with hostile fire
and our men were beginning to fall, but
this disturbed us less than the confusing
orders which sent us now this way,
now that. It seemed as though the
regiment was doomed to disgrace, if
not to destruction. Then it was that
we discovered the heroic character of
our lieutenant-colonel. Ignoring his
incompetent and now helpless superior,
he calmly assumed command and there,

in the face of the enemy's fierce fire
halted us, re-formed our disordered line
and led us forward once more.   There
was no lack of courage in the men ;
they were willing to do all that could
be asked of them.   Throughout the
remainder of that deadly though glorious charge the regiment proved that
all it needed was what it had at last
found — a true leader.   We gained the
crest of the hills along with the rest of
the column.   Our first real battle was
fought.   We had come through it, not
indeed faultlessly — few new regiments
ever do that — but so that we could
look with reverence upon our torn flag,
and view our sadly thinned ranks with
sorrow but without shame.   Not perfectly, yet not unworthily we had endured the ordeal of battle.

In seven months the regiment, which
left home little better than a mob save
for the character of its members and the

spirit which animated it, had become a battalion of seasoned and well-officered soldiers fit to take its place in a brigade of veterans. We had learned to wear the armour so hastily put on. We had fitted ourselves to it.

If the story of the making of this regiment is worth the telling, that is not because it is in any way exceptional but because it is typical. Some regiments were more fortunate than ours in their first commanders; some met the test of battle sooner. Details vary, yet the process through which we went is a fair example of that by which hundreds of thousands of peaceful American citizens were transformed into the soldiers of one of the most formidable armies of history. The process was not ideal; it was in many ways illogical, unmilitary and wasteful; yet its results have seldom been surpassed.

The Household of the Hundred Thousand

THE site of the old home camp, the first mustering ground of many regiments, is now covered with pretty suburban homes about which I sometimes think, the ghosts of war times must play at midnight.

For us young fellows it was a rude beginning of real life when we found ourselves inside the great board fence and line of sentries which enclosed the rows of rough, wooden barracks. The members of our own company were indeed mostly neighbours, their faces were familiar, we had grown up together; yet never before had we been thrown into such intimate association. It is one thing to meet a man every day on the street or even at work ; it is quite another to be compelled to bunk with him and take your breakfast out of the same camp-kettle. For the youth who had been kept in a glass case at home this experience was trying and often disastrous, but for the most of us it was wholesome. We learned our own hitherto-unsuspected faults, we discovered the good qualities of even our most faulty comrades, we saw human nature at close range.

Even the officers could not escape the influence of this enforced commingling. They had, indeed, separate quarters and their own mess ; they stood also on a vantage ground of almost despotic authority, for from the moment when we were mustered into service we were subject to the same military law which governed the regular army.

But drawn as our officers were from the same mass, knowing their men for old neighbours, often for intimate friends, frequently for those who had been at least their social equals they could not hold themselves far aloof, and few of them cared to do so. They could form no separate caste and this, perhaps, had its disadvantages; but for these there were certainly large compensations. It became necessary for an officer to prove his right to rank by qualities of leadership. The best officers were those who, without sacrifice of dignity kept a lively sense of comradeship with their men.

The work of drill began before we received either arms or uniforms, and from the very first we managed to go through with that essential of camp life, the evening dress parade. Then the grounds would be filled with spectators, mostly home friends : fathers, mothers, wives, sisters and sweethearts, bringing with them dainties to supplement what seemed to them the hard fare of camp. We lived well and were not a little spoiled in those days; and when we departed for the front, the mistaken kindness of those who loved us loaded us down with all sorts of knick-knacks for comfort and convenience. Though loath to part with these, our first marching days made us more loath to carry them. When a man's back becomes his only storehouse, he soon finds that riches do not consist in the abundance of the things which he possesses. Patent writing-cases, extra socks and mittens, "ponchos" for the shoulders, "havelocks" for the head, etc., etc., began to strew the road, and in a short time we were reduced to an absolutely socialistic equality in this world's goods. Whatever differences remained were those purely personal ones which can be discovered only by experience of each other's ways and characters.

In a regiment of a thousand men any extensive acquaintance outside one's own company comes slowly; yet many things served to bring us into fellowship. There was little clannishness, every man in blue was a comrade; yet, after all, each company was a family by itself, and in the company little coteries collected like the eddies in a river pool.

On the march two men usually tented together. In camp, when logs or brush were available, four could use their tent pieces to better advantage than two or three, and the camp was thus made more compact.

Men came together as tent-mates by a process of natural or social selection. They had been schoolmates or work-fellows in the same shop, perhaps they were related as brothers or cousins, or they had been near neighbours and old friends. So it was at first; but new experiences in toil and peril were often solvents out of which new associations crystallised. Kindred spirits found each other; more and more the company became a greater family within which lesser and more intimate families grew up. Sometimes there were disagreements which broke up first arrangements; but commonly a quiet, almost unnoticed attraction of affinity drew the final groups together in bonds seldom broken save by death or disabling wounds or sickness. A few of these soldierly friendships bind old men even to-day; many more are cherished by lonely survivors as memories too sacred for common talk.

When for months you and your comrade have slept at night under one blanket and shared each other's daily bread, even though it were but hardtack; when you have learned to depend on him and he upon you for help in trouble or comfort in sickness; when together you have entered the hell of deadly battle — after which the first question would be: " Is Joe safe ? " " Where is Sam ? "   " Is little Gus alive ? " — when together you have suffered hunger, thirst, heart-breaking weariness; above all, when, huddled together in storm or cold you have had to endure long days of dreary, monotonous, comfortless idleness then you know what it means to live a common life with a fellow-man; and if he and you meet the test, then you know what friendship means.

In the routine of camp life the music of drum and fife was conspicuously audible. We were wakened at daybreak by the shrill tune of the reveille; the last sound at night was that of the drum perambulating the camp with " taps," commanding " lights out " and sleep;

while all day long frequent summons to varied duties came by "call" of drum and fife. There was " sick call," which brought all the indisposed who were able to walk into forlorn squads to be conducted by the orderly ser- jeants to the surgeon's tent for treat- ment. Its absurdly merry notes seemed to say :

> "Come to the Doctor's
> And get your castor oil."

Then "guard call," inevitable as the day, but always unwelcome. Drill call or "assembly" meant simply our daily work. At dress parade, which closed the day's active duties, the band dis- coursed its most martial strains, and after supper we heard it once more in the pleasant tones of "retreat,' and later of "tattoo" the music of which comes most impressively into recollec- tion. From one camp after another the measured minor strains would sound

forth ; from near and far, from camps
away beyond our sight, it would melt
into distance, and then beyond the
westward woods the artillery bugles
would take it up until it died away
with their mellow notes. It was the
voice of the comradeship of a mighty,
invisible host.

One can readily understand how per-
sistently, how intimately this music of
drum and fife wove itself into our lives.
Some of those queer, old-fashioned, half-
melancholy, half-merry tunes sing themselves in my memory even now.

What of the band in the day of
battle ? Was not martial music the
soldier's inspiration ? Did we not
charge to its thrilling strains? We did
nothing of the kind. There was other
work for the musicians. On the ap-
proach of battle they were always sent
to the rear for duty as stretcher-bearers
and helpers in the field hospital. One

pretty sure sign that bloody work was before us was the disappearance of the band; and the grimmest, most sickening, yet most merciful work of war was theirs at such times.

In active campaigning, our camps were apt to be hasty, though never disorderly bivouacs, and even if a few days' halt were made and the camp duly formed, rest for weary and footsore men took precedence of drill and, in fact, of everything not absolutely necessary. But one thing was inevitable as day and night. This was roll-call. In storm or sunshine, in camp or on the march, before and after battle, the first thing in the morning and the last at night, we had to answer to our names. The first serjeant calls the roll. He knows the list by heart, and calls it off without book, in the dark if need be.

At first irritatingly suggestive of that

more than schoolboy tutelage which is one penalty of a soldier's life, the morning and evening roll-call by its insistent monotony gradually grew into an accepted item of existence, like salt pork and hard-tack.   But when exposure, toil, and battle began to thin the ranks, the roll-call gained a new meaning; it became a none too oft-repeated personal history of our lives, a daily bulletin of passing events and a reminder of those already past.   It told of the sick and disabled, of those fallen out by the way, prisoners perhaps in the hands of the enemy, here and there of one promoted, here and there of one dead.   There were days when those of us who could answer to our names did so with a feeling of solemn thankfulness and other days when the omission, or perhaps the inadvertent calling of a name sent a rush of sad remembrance through the ranks.

Imagine, if you can, the roll-call at night after a day of battle! — the mustering of the thinned company in the darkness; the suspense as the familiar names are spoken — it may be by an unfamiliar voice, for in battle death seemed to seek and find the serjeants; the frequent pauses for inquiry; perhaps the answer of a comrade for one who has fallen, perhaps a mournful silence. Oh, those silent names! For days, yes, for weeks and months every now and then you seem to hear them at evening roll-call, and somewhere, close beside you it may be, an unseen presence seems to whisper: "Here!"

I think all who passed through it remember the winter of the Fredericksburg campaign with a shudder. Preceding the battle came freezing nights with thawing days, rain-soaked or snow-bound camps; days when our little tents were first buried in the snow, then frozen so stiff that when marching orders came we could scarcely strike or fold them; then short but horrible marches through slush and mud with our doubly-heavy half-frozen loads; scanty rations withal because of delayed supply trains: a month of exposure, discomfort, and misery.

The like of this is, however, what soldiers must expect, and if victory had come at the end we could have borne far worse hardship cheerfully. But the ciimax was the slaughter at Fredericksburg. The sting of that defeat was felt not as a dishonour, but as undeserved disaster. We knew that courage and devotion such as any people might be proud of had been uselessly sacrificed. Yet the gloom of those winter days after the battle was not that of despair; it was the bitter prospect of indefinitely prolonged struggle, an outlook dark indeed to men who were soldiers not for glory but only for home and country.

The depression of that time was doubtless responsible for at least as large a loss of life as the battle beside the river. Hardship and exposure had bred sickness, and the mood of the hour offered feeble resistance to death. For months the little funeral processions were mournfully frequent; from our own brigade alone there were often two or three in a day.

There are no funerals on the march; there are none after battle. On the march, if a man falls out of the ranks stricken with mortal sickness or exhaustion he is left to be picked up by the ambulance, perhaps to die alone by the way. The column cannot halt. After battle, there are but ghoulish burials. But in settled camp the decencies of death are rudely observed.

The first funeral in our company

was that of one of our serjeants, a
young man whom we all loved. He
died shortly after Christmas-time. A
box of good things from home had
lately arrived; out of the boards of
that box we managed to make a coffin
for our dear comrade and the whole
company marched to his grave. But
the most of our dead were buried without coffin and funerals became too
common for any but scantiest ceremony.
A drum and fife playing the Dead
March, a firing squad of three to give
a parting volley over the grave, then
the chaplain, then the body of the dead
soldier wrapped in his blanket and
carried on a stretcher by two men
followed perhaps by half-a-dozen intimate friends, and that was all.

In the brigade graveyard at the top
of the hill which grew so dismally in
population during the winter, there
were no headstones — only little pine

8

boards torn from empty cracker-boxes, with the name of the departed written thereon in lead pencil or cut in with a jack-knife. I remember several head-boards hewn from cedar, the most lasting of woods, made with great care and pains, with deep-cut inscriptions. These, you may be sure were stronger proof of true affection than many of the costly monuments which challenge the beholder's eye in our great cemeteries.

It is a pathetic fact that all through the war many men who might have recovered from the fevers and other ailments common to a soldier's life died because homesickness had quenched their power of resistance to disease. Indeed there were not a few deaths from homesickness pure and simple. It is not a complaint recognised in official reports, but ask any army surgeon and he will probably tell you some surprisingly sad tales.

Fatal cases were, however, exceptional, though the ordinary malady was
common enough. Sometimes its mani-
festations were serio-comic, as for instance in my own case.

In the midst of our worst other dis-
comforts, we were for a time compelled
to subsist upon ancient hard-tack, which
was often in such condition that, "if
you called, it would come to you;" and
one day I strolled off alone into the
woods beyond the camp and sitting
on a log, gave myself to meditation. I
thought of my privations, not bitterly,
but with a deliberate and curiously an-
alytical wonder. I said to myself:
"How much more a man can stand
than he would have believed possible!"
Then my thoughts wandered to my
far-away home with its simple luxuries
and comforts, and that which came
most vividly to mind was the fact that
once — it seemed ages ago — I had

really had good, wholesome soft bread to eat every day, and three times a day at that! I then began to ask myself: "Would I ever again have soft bread every day?" "Was it possible that such happiness could be mine?" And I said to myself dolefully: "No! It is not likely. You are a soldier; you can henceforth have only soldier's fare; you will probably fill a soldier's grave. You will never taste soft bread again!"

Now this may seem absurd in the telling, yet God knows it was horribly real at the time.

But this was only a passing mood with the mass of us. We were a host of young men; life was too strong and elastic for even the depression which followed Fredericksburg to hold us down. We found ways to amuse ourselves.

One of the frequent but evanescent snow-storms of that semi-southern land had fallen, and snowballing became a common sport. Finally an organised contest was proposed between our regiment and two others of the brigade. We were so much stronger in numbers than the older regiments that this apparently one-sided arrangement only equalised forces, and as an offset we were given the doubtful advantage of the defensive. Both sides were drawn up in rigid military array with officers in their places of command. As for ourselves, we made piles of snowballs and awaited the onset. It came like a whirlwind; those veterans had not been through a dozen real battles for nothing, and as their line approached and the missiles began to fly, it was like a hailstorm. The snowballs were wet and hard, often icy; both sides were in hot earnest and like the ancient Romans we aimed at the faces of our foes. I hardly know how it all looked for I was in the thick of it and almost blinded, but I know how it felt. If the snowballs had been bullets, I should have been riddled from head to foot.

We stood our ground manfully for a little while; but the too subtle strategy of our commander had divided our force; we were outnumbered at the critical point and the superior discipline of our opponents prevailed. We had to confess ourselves beaten; and from the way our veteran friends crowed over us I almost think they were tempted to inscribe that snowball victory on their battle-flags.

An even better antidote for the blues was the work which became necessary as the army went into winter quarters. There is no pleasanter occupation than home building, be it ever so rude, and we took much pains and found great enjoyment in the making and furnishing of our little houses. Some regiments whose location was near suitable timber built good-sized log huts ; we were compelled to be more modest. The dwelling which my own group of four tent-mates erected and occupied may serve as a fair example. Four pieces of shelter tent buttoned together made the roof which covered a log structure twelve feet long and five or six feet wide. The log walls were about three feet high ; but as the ground sloped away from the company street we dug out the rear half of our hut, and there we had a little room in which we could stand erect. This served for our kitchen. The more elevated part was occupied by a broad bed of poles covered with dried grass and our blankets. This made a springy couch on which the four of us could sleep comfortably side by side ; and the edge of the bed was just high enough to make a convenient seat with our feet resting on the kitchen floor. About the sides of the house were shelves and pegs for our belongings.

In the kitchen end, beside the door, we built a fireplace and chimney. Now a wooden fireplace and chimney may seem ludicrously impractical, yet that is what we and thousands of others actually built from green pine sticks. But we fireproofed it with a coating of clay on the inside, and it answered its purpose perfectly. It "drew" finely and gave us no end of solid comfort. Some of the chimneys did not work so well and then the draught was increased by the precarious expedient of an empty, headless barrel placed on top. This generally served for a short time; but the barrel was pretty sure to take fire and then there would be a grand excitement and much merriment over the frantic effort to extinguish the blaze.

Not the chimneys alone played tricks

on the householders. Mischievous comrades have been known to drop a handful of cartridges down a chimney from the outside, with the result of a smothered explosion and a great scattering of ashes and embers over everything and everybody within.

The spirit of fun also found outlet in the adornment of the gables of our dwellings with various legends suggestive of the personal peculiarities of the inmates. For instance, of two queerly assorted tent-mates, one had been a church sexton and a conspicuous functionary at village funerals ; the other had worked in a silverware factory. Over their door some wag tacked a sign with the inscription :

DOWD AND GRIFFITH,

JEWELLERS AND UNDERTAKERS.

As few of us were content with the wholesale and not too dainty work of the company cooks, we did most of our cooking ourselves by our kitchen fires, and those of us who survived the war learned enough to make us useful to the women who were wise enough to choose us as husbands, though I fear the details of our housekeeping would have shocked them.

Many a pleasant evening we spent about our little fireplace. We talked about home, the girls we loved, relig-ion, politics, literature, camp gossip, everything. Or we read, when we had books or papers from home, or wrote letters or our journals.

There was, however, little real pri-vacy in those huts so close together with their canvas roofs. Any loud talk could be heard from one to the other and in the evening after " re-treat " the camp became a very babel of men singing, talking, laughing, swear-ing, telling stories; a chorus in one tent, a game of cards in another; in three or four at once loud discussions of the doings in the regiment or of the state of the country.

At nine o'clock " taps " sounded, and the officer of the day went the rounds to see that all lights were out. This was early bed-time in the long winter nights, and by various ruses we managed to conceal the glimmer of candles re-lighted after the officer had returned to the guard-house. The Bible and Shakespeare were responsible for some of these evasions of military regulations, quiet little games of cards for more of them.

Speaking of cards and Bibles brings up the image of the chaplain.

A friend in a regiment distinguished for its high discipline and its severe losses in many battles said to me one day: " A good chaplain makes a good regiment." Then, in illustration he told me the story of their own chaplain, a man of fine culture, high social position and great devotion to his calling. In his pastoral visits through the camp if he surprised a group engaged in a game of " bluff," he would quietly scoop up the stakes, put the money in his own pocket and say : " Boys, this is for the hospital fund." Strange to say, the boys never murmured. The cheerful but shamefaced reply was always, " All right, chaplain."

I think no one will wonder who hears the rest of the story.

On the eve of battle this chaplain took personal command of the stretcher-bearers and when the combat was raging he would lead his little band of helpers into the thickest fire to succour the wounded. My friend told me : " I have known him to creep out between the opposing lines to bring off wounded men. The boys all knew that if they got into trouble, Chaplain H—— would be there to help if this was in the power of mortal man." There were other chaplains of like spirit. Our own was not only untiring in his care for the sick and wounded in the hospitals, but always ready for any kindly service he could render to the members of the regiment or to their families at home. But it must be confessed that they were not all of this stamp. It was quite possible for the chaplain to be the most useless officer in a regiment.

It could not be said of our regiment that we were like the men of Cromwell's " new model," yet we came from communities in which Puritanism was traditional and in almost every company there were at least a few examples of strong Christian character. The two serjeants in our own company who died in the service, one by sickness and the other in battle were men of this sort, and one of our captains who fell in battle was a man whose Christian life was a benediction to the regiment.

But occasionally one met with what good people might consider strange inconsistencies. I have heard swearing euphemistically described as the utterance of "short prayers." One of our field officers was a man whose godly life was known to all, yet in intense moments short prayers of startling character would escape him.

On a Sunday, so it was said, a group of officers gathered in his tent fell into warm discussion of some troublesome regimental affair. The lieutenant colonel paced back and forth with his hands behind him taking no part in the conversation but biting his bristly moustache, as was his wont when annoyed. Suddenly he stopped short and, facing them exclaimed: "Well, gentlemen, let's stop this damned quibbling and go

and worship God awhile." Then pick-
ing up his Bible he strode off by himself
into the woods, leaving his guests to
their reflections.

Religious men were apt to be more
intense in the army than at home, and
those who frequented the prayer-meet-
ings in the tents or, in pleasant weather,
under the trees, will never forget their
atmosphere of warm and solemn earnest-
ness.

On the night before we stormed
Marye's Hill the moon shone through
fleecy clouds and it was only partly
dark. We lay in line of battle at rest,
the most of us trying to sleep. Presently, out toward the front between
us and the skirmish line voices were
heard. The watchful major anxiously
asked: "What is that? Who is talking out there?" One of the men
answered, "Major, it is only some of
the boys having a prayer-meeting;"

and the major says that instantly, in place of his fears and vexation, a feeling of deep thankfulness came over him as he thought of the prayers ascending for us all on the verge of battle.

There was a young soldier in our company to whom his mother, when she parted from him, gave a little book of daily Scripture selections. She said to him : " I have another just like this and we will both read the same verses every day." The soldier kept true tryst with his absent mother and, no matter where he was read his text every day. As we lay in the sunken road on that fateful morning after the moonlight prayer-meeting and the bullets began to speak their deadly whispers in our ears and we were all feeling the chill and dread of the plunge into battle, he opened his little book. The text for the day was, " Fear not, for I am with thee : be not dismayed, for I am thy

God ! " He has told me that if a voice from heaven had spoken it could not have been more clear, and for the remainder of that terrible day all fear was gone.

We believed in our cause, in the war, and in final victory ; but we were not soldiers for the love of it. The end of fighting and *home* was the goal of the hope of the army — a vain hope to thousands of us, yet the star that beckoned us all forward. How eagerly our thoughts turned northward might be seen on mail days. Letters came with varying regularity ; in settled camp we could generally count on them, but in times of active campaign mails were uncertain and when one arrived it was pathetic to see the wave of expectation that would sweep through the ranks. Often a cheer would go up when the postman with mail bags slung across his horse, came in sight. Then there was impatient waiting until the letters for the company came down from head-quarters and an anxious crowd around the captain as he called them off. The disappointment of those who received none was often pitiful. You would hear one and another say: " Captain, is n't there one for me? " " Captain, are you sure? I know I ought to have one this time."

Then, tired and hungry as we were after the day's march, supper would go untasted until we could read the news from home; and long afterward by our camp-fires we would talk it over; and you might hear letterless Tom come to Bill and ask, " What does your wife say about my folks? Has she seen them lately? Are they all well? " The most of us would read our letters with quiet gladness; but now and then you might see some poor fellow bending with tear-stained face over his message from home and hear his comrades saying in hushed tones of sympathy, " Jim has bad news ; his little girl is dead."

The outgoing mail was far lighter than the incoming : we wrote under difficulties ; yet there were times when the whole camp seemed filled with scribes. But our letters were apt to be brief, and when any important movement was at hand we knew that they would not be promptly forwarded. Inconvenient information sometimes travelled in army letters.

Our turn at picket duty was, with some of us, a favourite time for writing up our correspondence. In pleasant weather it was only at the outposts that the work was trying. "On the reserve," or even " the support," we had only to hold ourselves in readiness for emergencies. Picket duty was often a positively enjoyable change from the monotony of camp. When fires were allowed we would fell great oaks for the mere fun of it, cut off their tops and branches for our fire and let the trunks lie. War is wasteful in ways little thought of. Yet the scars of the picket posts were as nothing compared with the deserts made by the great camps.

But picket duty must be done regardless of weather, and at the outposts no fires were permitted at any time. I remember once leaving camp in a snowstorm which, by the time we reached our post had changed into a cold rain. Night was falling, we had no tents, none were allowed on the picket line; but a German comrade and I managed to prop up a rubber blanket upon sticks so that it gave a scanty shelter from the rain, and as we crept under it my friend exclaimed, " Ach, here dees is nice under an injun-rubber himmel ! "

Some of the nights on the picket line will always dwell in my memory. There

was one when our post was in the heart
of a forest of giant pines.   A wild north-
wester was blowing and its elfin music
roared among the tree-tops as if the
myriad spirits of the power of the air
were let loose.   Yet down below where
we stood, all was peace ; not a breath
stirred the feathery branches or the soft
carpet of pine-needles under our feet.
Even now I can feel the deep and
solemn repose, the sense of mighty,
restful shelter from the war of elements
with which the shadowy forest pillars
enwrapped us.

During our winter in camp along the
Rappahannock the only danger on the
picket line was from bushwhackers.
But nothing is more trying to the nerves
than the chance of being picked off in
the dark by unseen skulkers.   In the
face of the enemy it is different: you
then expect to be shot at and to shoot.
It is far more dangerous, but scarcely

less exciting. Soldiers are not fond of picket work, but they hate the monotonous restraint and night work of ordinary and yet perfectly safe camp-guard duty. A common punishment for slight delinquencies is to give a man an extra turn on guard. Severe punishments, such as " ball and chain," or even tying a man up by the thumbs so that his feet barely touch the ground were not uncommon, though I am glad to say that this cruel torture was never permitted in our own and many other regiments.

One night I was serjeant of the guard at brigade headquarters. The guard-house was a log building divided by a loosely built partition with wide crevices into two rooms : one for the guard, the other for a prison, in which at that time three deserters were confined. My duty compelled me to keep awake, and the prisoners, with the shadow of the death-penalty upon them spent the whole night in talk.

Without heeding the guard, they laid bare their lives to each other as men will sometimes do when the end seems near. They talked about their families — one at least was a married man — and about the doings of younger days when they were boys on the farm, and they seemed to hunt out every bit of wrong or shame in their lives as though it must be confessed, at least to each other. One of them was evidently a very decent man; but another, who had been a serjeant in his regiment and plainly the ring-leader, was, judging from his talk a desperado. Once, after he had told of some wild deed he said: "But I have done worse things than that; things that would hang me if they were known." Then, in answer to an inquiry of his companions: "No, I won't tell you even now about that."

In the morning I saw this man. He was strikingly handsome, a most soldierly-looking fellow. He talked with me freely and pleasantly; there was something fascinating about him.

The deserters were not shot. With sentence suspended they were replaced in the ranks and told that, if they did their duty the next time their regiment was called into action, they would be pardoned.

Shortly afterward came the bloody but brilliant little battle at Franklin's Crossing. In the first boat which left the shore — the same in which our noble Captain D—— was killed — was the dare-devil ex-serjeant. Before the boat reached the opposite bank he was out of it, and without waiting for any one, he rushed straight at the enemy's earthwork alone. We expected to see him drop, but he bore a charmed life; he was one of the first to enter the works, and by sheer boldness he brought off half-a-dozen prisoners and coolly marched them before him to the rear.

We never saw a military execution; but that which I remember as the saddest scene of our army life was the degradation of an officer. He had been condemned for cowardice before the enemy.

The division was drawn up in a great hollow square, and the officer in full uniform was marched under guard into the centre where all could see him. There in loud tones the finding of the court-martial and its sentence were read, after which the adjutant approached the condemned officer, tore off his shoulder-straps, took his sword from him, ran it half way into the ground and broke it before his face. The guard then closed about the disgraced and degraded man and marched him away.

I had never seen him before — he

was from another brigade — but as he passed near and I could look into the deathly pale face of that young man with the heart-break of despair written on every feature, I said to myself, " This is a hundred times worse than death "; and I found myself wildly wishing that he had been shot dead in battle ! When the parade was dismissed we went back to our quarters in awe-struck silence, broken only by expressions of deep compassion.

In strong contrast with this, the grandest and most impressive scene we witnessed was the review of the army by President Lincoln.

It was on a dull wintry day. We marched several miles from our camp before we came, early in the morning to the reviewing ground, which was a vast, desolate, open space, mostly level but with little hillocks here and there. Upon one of these we halted waiting for the mustering of the gathering host. For hours the dark lines of men in blue poured in from every direction until all the plain and every little hilltop was alive with them.

For six or seven months we had been members of the great army; we had shared its toils and perils, we had lived its life, we had felt the throbbing of its mighty pulse in our own blood, we had been part of its long line of battle; yet we had never as yet seen the assembly of our brethren in arms. Now the plain was growing black with them; a hundred thousand men were forming in apparently solid masses, the battle-flags of the regiments waving close together.

The scene was the more impressive because there were no idle spectators. This was no gala day for curious, gazing, merry-making crowds, and brilliant costumes, and feasting and huzzas; but solemnly, silently save for the measured tramp of battalions and the rolling of the drums a nation's strength was massing as if to weigh itself, to feel itself and ask its own soul if it were fit for the mighty work and the awful sacrifices awaiting it.

We could not know then that Chancellorsville, Gettysburg, the Wilderness, Spottsylvania, Cold Harbor, Petersburg, written across the scroll of a short two years to come were holding in their fateful though glorious names the doom of death or wounds for more in number than all the thousands of us who beheld each other that day. But we felt that a heavy-laden future was swiftly coming toward us; we could almost hear the rustling of her wings in the air of the leaden sky under which, apart from the world, alone with ourselves and God, we stood a great brotherhood of consecrated service.

But now our moment has come. We take our place in the moving ranks. We marched in close column with double company front, so that each regiment took up small space. As we neared the reviewing stand the tall figure of Lincoln loomed up. He was on horseback and his severely plain, black citizen's dress set him in bold relief against the crowd of generals in full uniform grouped behind him. Distinguished men were among them; but we had no eyes save for our revered President, the Commander-in-Chief of the Army, the brother of every soldier, the great leader of a nation in its hour of trial. There was no time save for a marching salute; the occasion called for no cheers. Self-examination, not glorification had brought the army and its chief together; but we passed close to him so that he could look into our faces and we into his.

None of us to our dying day can forget that countenance! From its presence we marched directly onward toward our camp and as soon as " route step " was ordered and the men were free to talk they spoke thus to each other : " Did you ever see such a look on any man's face ? " " He is bearing the burdens of the nation." " It is an awful load ; it is killing him." " Yes, that is so ; he is not long for this world ! "

Concentrated in that one great, strong yet tender face, the agony of the life or death struggle of the hour was revealed as we had never seen it before. With new understanding we knew why we were soldiers.

A Little Battle

THE great battles of a war like ours absorb the attention of historians; yet scattered between these grand climacterics, like local squalls or thunder-showers in the intervals of sweeping storms, there were hundreds of little, unrecorded fights which, to those who felt their fury often meant almost as much as the main tempests.

We found it so in the very last affair in which our regiment took part. Our term of service was all but ended. The men who had been detailed as clerks at headquarters, teamsters, ambulance drivers etc., had been sent back to their companies in anticipation of our speedy mustering out; everything seemed quiet along the Rappahannock; we reckoned our battles all fought and dared at last to believe that home-going for those who were left of us was actually a possibility. "Home again!" — it was all we talked of by day, it coloured our dreams by night as we slept in our pleasant camp under the summer moon.

When therefore, early on a June morning the command came to strike tents and prepare to move, a thrill of expectation went with it through the regiment. But our vision of home quickly melted as we saw the stir of preparation spreading like an advancing wave into all the regiments about us, and its last pathetic remnants were rudely blotted out by the distribution of the ominous twenty extra rounds of cartridge. We handled them gingerly, none too willingly, for they said to us, "Not home this time, boys, — battle once more first; some of you will never see home."

Late in the afternoon a short march brought our division to the hills above the fateful river; for the third time we beheld sleepy old Fredericksburg away at our right, and directly before us the familiar amphitheatre of fields shut in by distant hills. It seemed incredible that twice within six months trampling armies had here been locked in the bloody embrace of mighty battle; no more peaceful sight could be imagined than those gently rolling, grassy plains with their crown of wooded, leafy upland all bathed in the slanting rays of sweet June afternoon sunshine.

A single suspicious blot marred the landscape. Opposite where we stood, at the farther side of the river guarding our old crossing place, the yellow mound of a freshly dug earthwork loomed up; yet for all we could see it might have been a great grave, so silent, so apparently lifeless was it.

But there was no lingering for the view. Down the hill we went, out over the level ground beneath, and from every side we could see the dark lines pouring over the slopes until, with swift and silent precision the division was formed in battle array. In a few moments as if by magic the northern side of the river valley had become alive with the presence of a sternly-marshalled host.

The southern side also awoke. Out from a distant grove a Confederate regiment, the support of the as-yet-invisible picket line came forth. We could see the sheen of their rifles flashing in the sunshine as they hastened toward the earthwork.

As yet not a shot had been fired and scarce a sound was heard; even the tramp of marching feet and the

rumble of artillery wheels was muffled
by the soft, grassy ground. I can feel
even now the queer sensation of un-
reality, as though it were all a gigantic
pantomime, or some eerie flitting of
armies of ghosts.

But appearances could not deceive
us. We knew too well the Spirit of
the Place; we waited its arousal with
grave expectation. The feeling in our
ranks was picturesquely expressed by
a stuttering little fellow in our company when, as we halted for a few moments on the hills above and watched
the silent river and apparently-deserted
plain and hills, some one ventured
the rash opinion that the enemy had
decamped. The stammerer quickly replied:

"You j-just g-g-go ov-ver and s-stir
up the hive, and the b-b-bees will c-come
out f-fast enough!"

That river had always been a River

of Death whenever we had crossed it. Were we to prove it once more? The question in our hearts was answered when the pontoon train with its long line of great boat-laden waggons issued from our ranks and, like an enormous snake began to wind its way toward the river, its head plunging downwards and disappearing in the hidden road leading to the water's edge. Pontoons at the front always meant bloody business in those Rappahannock days. The illusion, the silence before the storm, is at an end. Hark! There is a rattle of rifles from the other side. With it another clatter and roar, as from our side three batteries gallop forth, wheel near the edge of the ravine in which the river flows, unlimber, and quicker than it takes to tell, crash! crash! crash! the volleys from eighteen cannon rend the evening air. Through sudden clouds of white smoke red flashes dart like savage tongues of wild beasts, the gunners leap like demons to and fro in apparent fury, yet really with mechanical precision as they load and fire, reload and fire again. A little breeze lifts the veil of smoke, through the rift we catch a glimpse of the earthwork beyond the river; it is an inferno of bursting shells and clouds of dust. Woe to the men behind that torn and fire-scorched mound! We knew there could be but few of them at most; they had no artillery with which to answer ours, it seemed in truth like crushing mosquitoes with a sledge-hammer. Yet the crossing of a deep river in face of even a few determined opposers is always a ticklish piece of work and our commander meant to take no chances. The thunderous strokes of eighteen cannon are not too much to make the task of the engineers who must lay the bridge a safe one; whether even such ponderous defence is sufficient we are soon to see.

Our attention had been riveted upon the scene before us and we failed to notice that our colonel had been called away by a message from the commander of the brigade, but as he galloped back one look into his grave, determined face was enough. We knew what was coming before the sharp command rang out. " Attention, battalion! Forward, double quick, march!"

In battle, events arrive suddenly. You learn to expect it thus, yet like the final summons to a slowly dying man the order which sends you into the vortex of fire is apt to come with a shock of surprise. To us at that moment the surprise was the more keen because home-going instead of battle had so lately been our prospect, and least of all had we dreamed that, out of a dozen regiments we would be the first called upon for specially perilous duty.   But that curious electric thrill which comes with the battle order, which merges your individual consciousness into the composite consciousness of a regiment sent us forward, and before we could fairly ask ourselves what it all meant, we were swiftly moving toward the river by the road over which the pontoons had passed.   We had travelled that road before, we knew it well.   At the edge of the plateau it turns sharply and descends by a dug way in the steep bank parallel with the stream to a small piece of open level ground close by the water; and when we reached the turn of the road where we could look down, a glance showed what the din of the cannonade had concealed. The earthwork was but part of the defence of the crossing. Below the line of our battery fire, out of reach of its shells, was a row of rifle-pits manned by sharpshooters who were doing deadly work. A few of the pontoon boats were on the ground close to the water, but none of them were launched; the train was in disorder, the engineers were being shot down at every attempt to handle their boats and our task was clearly before us. With another regiment from the brigade which was coming down by a different route through a little ravine, we must force the passage of the river. It began to be hot work as soon as we reached the dug way. Even now I can hear the waspish buzz of bullets, and feel the sting of the gravel sent into my face, as they rip through the ground at my feet. It was hotter still on the little flat when two regiments quickly arriving and huddled together with boats, waggons, and engineers, filled every inch of space. We could not return the enemy's fire and our closely packed crowd offered a pitifully easy mark for those sharpshooters only a hundred yards away.

But many strong hands were now heaving at the boats, in spite of the fire and of falling men, three or four of them were quickly launched. Then there is a moment of desperate confusion, no one responds to the frantic but unfamiliar orders of officers to " Get into those boats !" when out of the crowd one man springs forth, leaps to the gunwale of one of the boats and waving his gun high in the air cries, "Come on, boys!" It is Corporal Joe. Instantly the boat is filled, pushed off from the bank, and the engineers with their big oars begin to row out into the stream. Another boat quickly follows, and soon a flotilla of seven of these great scows, deeply laden, bristling with bayonets, is making such speed as is possible for such awkward craft toward the opposite shore. The bullets now patter like hail upon the water; a few strike the boats or the men in them, but the fire slackens as we near the bank. Our opposers were too few to resist us when once we landed, and they began to scatter. Some ran from the rifle-pits toward the earthwork, others disappeared through the bushes. Before the shore was fairly reached our men sprang out into the water and waded to the land, the boats were emptied quicker than they had been filled; no one paused to fire; there was a pell-mell rush of bayonet charge up the river bank straight at the earthwork. It was a race between our men and the Vermonters, and to this day it has been a matter of friendly dispute as to which regiment first entered the

enemy's works. But it was all quickly
over. The cannonade, which ceased
only when our charge began, had half
buried and almost wholly paralysed the
defenders of the little fort, only a few
feeble shots met us and we took nearly
eighty prisoners — all who were left
alive when we entered.

There were some ghastly sights inside that yellow mound. A Confederate officer, torn by one of our shells
lay dying; the captain of our company
sprang to his side, raised him tenderly,
gave him a drink from his canteen and
tried to soothe his passing moments.
But it was surprising how few of the
defenders had been killed. The worst
complaint of those brave men was that
they thought our batteries meant to
bury them alive!

We suffered far more severely. Our
own regiment lost nineteen, the engineers between thirty and forty, and the

Vermonters, who had come down to the river by a difficult though sheltered path, five or six : the cost of the crossing was between fifty and sixty men. I think it took not more than ten or fifteen minutes to fight our little battle, but those minutes were crowded with incidents. I have mentioned that of the dying Confederate officer. The handful of brave fellows who held that crossing so manfully, who made its conquest so dear to us, were heroes. We had naught but respect — nay, admiration — for them. It came to be always so. There was never a war fought more sternly, yet with less bitterness between those who met each other on bloody fields. Bank's Ford came only a month before Franklin's Crossing ; there, too, we took a number of prisoners. I shall never forget the talk with a group of them as we sat down together. If you could have seen us you would have found it hard to be-lieve that a few moments ago we had been firing into each other's faces. At the conclusion of our friendly chat, one of those Confederates said : —

" Well, boys, this war has got to be fought out. You must be good soldiers and do your duty, and we must do the same ! "

On our side two incidents were pa-thetic in their tragedy.

Among the killed was a private, a plain man to whom writing was a task. A few days before we marched he had managed to send a letter to his wife telling her that we would soon be at home. That was the last she heard from him, and when a few weeks later the regiment marched into the streets of his native city, the wife stood on the sidewalk waiting to welcome her husband. Some one had to take her away and tell her that he was dead.

Another of the killed was our senior
captain.   Before the days of labour
troubles, when master and men worked
side by side, he was owner of a manufactory, a man beloved by all his fellow-
citizens, and not least by the men who
worked under him.   He was near mid-
dle age, of peaceful tastes, without military aspirations, and enlisted only
because of a strong sense of duty.   He
knew his example would be followed,
he could multiply himself thus.   Work-
men and neighbours flocked about him;
he had been their captain in industry,
they made him their captain in war.
He might have been a field officer, but
he judged himself unfit.   To serve his
country where he could serve best was
his only ambition.   There were smarter
officers in the regiment, but none so beloved as this noble Christian the light
of whose example shone ever with
bright and benignant ray.

When we went down to the river
that day, Captain D——'s company
led the line and filled the first boat.
The enemy's fire was at its hottest
when they were shoved off.   Caring
always for others more than for himself, he commanded his men to lie down
and shelter themselves, but his perilous
duty was to direct the rowers and guide
the course of the fleet.   He stood up
to do it better.   The risk was fatal;
his commanding figure became the
mark for many rifles, and he fell before we were half way across.

Such a death for such a man was
nothing less than martyrdom, all the
harder because he knew that hundreds
of hearts were eagerly counting the
hours that lay between him and a joy-
ful welcome home.   But our dear captain was a type.   There were hundreds
like him in our army who never reached
home.

In the same boat with the heroic captain was a man from the other regiment who had been a deserter. His conduct in action was to determine his fate. How he managed to get into that first boat I do not know. He must have run far ahead of his own company, but when we neared shore he sprang out where the water was waist deep and, waiting for no one, charged alone up the bank. It looked like sure death ; but he escaped unhurt, and I believe was the very first to enter the enemy's works. Of course he secured his pardon.

In every battle there are a few heroes of the type with which Stephen Crane has made us familiar, whose ingenuity in finding safe places is amusing, and whose antics make life a burden to officers and file-closers. When we reached the boat-landing the ground was absolutely bare ; there was not a bush, or

tree, or rock ; the only possible shelter
from the leaden hail was a spring, — a
mere mud hole, perhaps three feet in
diameter. By lying down and curling
himself up in the mud and water a man
might fit into it. If the desirability of
land is the measure of its value, then
that mud hole was priceless, for it was
occupied every minute and each occu-
pant was envied by other would-be
tenants. As I came down the hill I
saw one of these fellows who had just
been routed out. A bullet had pierced
his arm as he rose from his muddy bed,
and he was dancing with pain, clasp-
ing his wounded arm with his unhurt hand and muttering angry curses
upon the officer who had disturbed
his repose. The vacant place was instantly taken by an old gray-bearded
fellow from my own company. Over
him stood the major, punching the
man with his sword, and accentuat-

ing each prod with an appropriate remark.

"Come, Peter [a prod], get out of this [prod]; your life is not worth any more than mine!" (final prod). And Peter slowly arose. It makes me laugh now, as it did then, to see his white, scared face gazing agape at the major, the mud and water dripping in festoons from his hair, his beard, and his clothes.

When we were half way across the stream a bullet struck the oar of one of our rowers, close to his hand with sharp ping and shock. For an instant the man seemed paralysed; he stopped rowing and our boat's head swung round, threatening collision with the craft beside us. In that other boat was a red-haired captain, a fiery little Irish gamecock. Quick as thought he grasped the situation, and leaning far over the gunwale with uplifted

sword, he hissed at the frightened
oarsman : —

"Row, damn you, or I'll cut your
head off!"

Never can I forget the appealing
glance of the poor fellow at that im-
pending sword, nor his sudden trans-
formation from helpless inertness to
desperate energy.

After the capture of the earthwork,
without waiting for the laying of the
bridge and the crossing of other troops,
our regiment was advanced in skirmish-
ing order far out across the plain, until
as night fell our line was established in
front of the ruins of the Bernard Mansion.   That night on the skirmish line
is one of the pleasantest memories of
my army life, but its story belongs
elsewhere.

The last fight of our regiment had
been fought.   We were proud of our
victory, and though the little battle is

barely noticed in military histories, it has an interest which makes it memorable to those who were there. It was the prelude of a great drama. The advance of our division of the Sixth Corps was a reconnaissance in force with the object of checking, if possible, Lee's northward movement, and in our little battle at Franklin's Crossing at the Rappahannock, the first blood of the great Gettysburg campaign was shed.

One Young Soldier

THE generous sentiment which would crown every one who fell in our Great War with the hero's wreath may be excessive, yet a personal acquaintance with almost any random portion of that enormous death-roll will certainly make one feel that its length is its least significance.

Not long ago I made a pilgrimage to my native village. Of course the old cemetery had to be visited. I knew the place was full of ghosts of other days, but a strange thrill went through me as I found the frequent stones inscribed with the names of former schoolmates or comrades who had fallen in the war.

Here was one that said, " Captain
R. S——, staff-officer — killed at the battle of the Wilderness." The silent stone
recalled dear friends and neighbours and
the sacrifice of their only son, the most
high-spirited and pluckiest young fellow
in the town, one of those ready and re-
sourceful characters to whom the word
"impossible" is a stranger. A little
farther on, under the shadow of ancient
cedars, were two marble shafts. One
bore the name of gentle, reticent, but
forceful W. P——, and the fateful words,
" Fell at the Battle of Bull Run."
How memory brings back the rush of
feeling with which the tidings of his
death came to us, his schoolmates from
whom he had so lately parted !

The other monument, in its simple
uprightness, seemed a fit memorial for
a knightly soul. Noble Harry B——!
We who knew him said to ourselves,
How can the world spare such as he !

But the legend on the marble told how
he met his death while in command of
a battery in Sheridan's great fight at
Cedar Creek.

I wandered on till I came to an hum-
ble stone whose rudely pathetic inscription, telling how it was " erected to his
memory by his wife," touched me
deeply. Bluff, hearty Henry H——was
one of my own company who fell on the
bloody field of Salem Heights.   Just a
plain man, only a private, no conspicuous hero, yet one of those faithfully
courageous souls who, when thick-flying
bullets are droning their deadly song,
and the scorching breath of battle tries
the line, never give captain or file-
closers a moment's anxiety. You could
always depend upon " Hank " to stand
like a rock with his face to the foe, and
to waste no shots on empty air. And
one reason for the Homeric deadliness of
our war was that both in the brown-clad

ranks of the Southrons and among the blue-coated Men of the North there were thousands like him.

I turned from the place in pensive mood. Remembering the awful harvest of great battle-fields I said to myself: Only a small fraction of it is planted in such peaceful places as this, yet this is a fair example of its lesson. Every village graveyard throughout our broad land tells the same story. Death waited with grim confidence for the choice spirits in that war, and the best of us who took our share in it are not those who live to tell its story.

Then thought travelled afar to the banks of the Rappahannock and its camps and battle-fields. I dreamed that once more I stood amid the familiar, blue-clad throng, yet there was a difference. Past and present seemed to mingle. Here and there a face would vanish or a well-remembered voice fail,

grow faint and far off, or suddenly become silent, and among these one, the
first sought for, the most desired, the
face and voice of my tent-mate.   I
awoke from my dream, remembering
that he, too, now belongs to the army
of the nobly fallen.

But ours was no common friendship.
We had been schoolmates before we became comrades, then tent-mates, finally
brothers like David and Jonathan.

We slept under one blanket; we
shared our rations and our confidences;
and if we did not fight side by side, that
was in part because he was corporal at
the right of the first platoon and my
place was at the other end of the line,
but also in part because he had a way
of doing such startlingly original things
in the face of danger.

His image rises before me now.
There he stands, tall, erect, balanced on
one foot while he nervously taps the

ground with the other and looks at
me with that mocking expression all
his own, that premonitory grin pro-
voked by some latent jest upon my
moralising.

This bantering trick, so common with
him, breaking out as it often did at
most unexpected and often atrociously
inappropriate moments, was an index of
the side of his character most open to
the general eye.   Joe was but eighteen
years old when he enlisted, just the
age when the boy is passing into the
man ; a good six feet in stature, without an ounce of spare flesh, long armed,
loose-jointed, at once too undeveloped
and too full of individuality to wear any
conventional garb with ease, so that
Uncle Sam's shop-made and ill-fitting
uniform hung upon his youthful but
powerful frame with anything but martial impressiveness.   This, however,
troubled him little.   An undue care for

appearance was never one of his foibles,
and the pomp and circumstance of war
always smote his keen Yankee sense of
the ludicrous. Yet he had withal the
manner and the heart of a gentleman,
and if you looked into those merry yet
piercing eyes, or listened for five minutes to the original ideas expressed by
that well modulated and pleasant voice
with just a suspicion of "away-down-
East" accent in it, you would be compelled to feel that in this boy there was
the making of no common man.

For a long time Joe was a puzzle to
his comrades. They could not understand why such a great boy, and one
too, so unmilitary in his ways, should
be a corporal. Some of the older men
resented it. And then, his persistent
practical joking, his careless independence and smiling indifference to rebuke
or criticism was perplexing, not to say
exasperating. Yet no one could posi-

tively dislike him.   He might be provoking at times, yet every one knew him
incapable of anything mean, and his
untiring good-nature and open-handed
generosity made warm friends for him
from the very start.

The captain certainly showed himself
a good judge of men when he made Joe
a corporal, though it took time to jus-
tify the choice, and the honours of office
sat but lightly upon the recipient.   Not
until our days of battle came did Joe
show any care for military distinction,
and he never bothered himself about
the promotion which others sought so
eagerly.

As everybody knows, the corporal's
rank is lowest in the company, only a
step above the position of a private, and
the distinguishing badge is that of the
"chevrons," two triangular stripes on
the sleeves of the coat.   So little did
Corporal Joe prize his office that he

would not at first wear these; but the
time speedily came when he found them
desirable. We were hurried into the
field, and when at Hagerstown in Maryland we joined the brigade to which we
were assigned, we found ourselves in
a strictly guarded camp. The men
were allowed to pass the gates only in
squads in charge of a non-commissioned
officer. And now Joe, seeing that the
chevrons might be useful, instead of
applying to the commissary for a regulation set, cut strips of light blue from
the skirt of his overcoat and rudely
sewed them on the sleeve of one arm
only. Then he proceeded to the gate
and attempted to pass the guard, who
of course stopped him.

"You have no non-commissioned
officer with you. Only a squad in
charge of a serjeant or corporal can
pass."

Joe held out the newly adorned

arm, exclaiming, " Is not *that* corporal enough for you ? "

The guard, a member of a veteran regiment, was perplexed yet obdurate.

" Yes, you may be a corporal, but where is your squad ? "

Quick as a flash Joe wheeled and showed the other, the plain coat-sleeve.

" There ! Is n't *that* squad enough for you ? "

And then the lieutenant in command of the guard, who had watched the whole performance broke into a hearty laugh and said, —

" You may pass. We will let you go as a non-commissioned squad."

It is to be feared that Joe was, for a long time, a thorn in the side of some of our company officers. Indeed I do not think that our orderly serjeant, a very business-like and soldierly German with a prejudice against the loose ways of our volunteer service, ever became reconciled to him.

We were a hastily enlisted regiment, and were rushed to the front and into active service imperfectly equipped. Our arms were at first old Harper's Ferry muskets with locks converted from flint to percussion. Want of respect for these antique weapons made us too careless of their condition : a grave military fault which was a grief and vexation to the orderly and also to our conscientious first lieutenant. At "inspection" one morning that officer found fault, justly enough, with Joe's gun. Taking it from its owner and holding it out before us all, he said sternly, —

" Corporal, what sort of an example is this to set before the company ? Look at the disgraceful condition of this musket ! — of what use would such a weapon be if we should be called into action ? "

With his peculiar and provoking grin, and in that bland and childlike tone which he assumed so readily, Joe impudently answered, —

"Why, lieutenant, if we get into a fight I expect to rely on my bayonet!"

Looking back upon this and similar incidents of our earlier service, I often wonder how Joe kept his chevrons at all. But when the stress of hard service came and we entered the toil and hardship of the march through the enemy's country, Joe's real quality began to make itself felt too strongly, both by men and officers, to make it worth while, or indeed safe, to notice his little irregularities; for whoever else lagged or straggled it was never Joe; no matter how dangerous or disagreeable the picket or fatigue duty he was never the one to shirk or complain. The officers found that for real service here was one man absolutely dependa-

ble; the men were braced by his cheerful
example, and they discovered moreover
that Joe was a good one to go to in
trouble. Had an improvident comrade
devoured his three days' rations prema-
turely? Joe was always ready to divide
his own remaining hard-tack. Was
some extra load to be carried, — an axe,
for instance? — he would cheerfully add
it to his own. A sort of admiration
for Joe began to appear, yet with reser-
vations. For one thing there was no
telling who would be the next victim of
one of his pranks. Bill B—— remem-
bers to this day how his supper was
spoiled one evening by Joe's ghastly
speculation about the method of the
fattening of our pork. And I remember a night on the picket reserve when
a circle of men lay asleep with their
feet toward the embers of a dying fire,
and Joe, ever-wakeful, quietly stealing
out of the group, gathered a mighty

armful of dry brush, gently deposited it upon the coals, and as the blaze mounted and the heat grew fierce, amused himself with the contortions of the roasted-out sleepers and with their drowsy profanity as they gradually awoke. He never swore himself, but I suspected at times that he took a sinful delight in the ingeniously blasphemous explosions of some of his comrades.

Then too, his ways were original. He had a genius for cookery, and the messes he concocted from meagre and sometimes unfamiliar materials were the wonder, and often the horror of his unsophisticated and conservative comrades; yet he was strangely fastidious withal. When a too greedy or too careless commissariat sent us boxes of ancient hard-tack, mementoes of last year's campaign, marked " White House " or "Harrison's Landing," whose mouldy

contents were living exponents of the
doctrine of evolution, Joe would not
eat a single cracker without careful dis-
section and removal of every inhabitant,
though we were near starving. And
though careless of outward appearances,
he was rigid in certain personal habits.
So the men thought when they saw
how, even in the dead of winter, he
would have his frequent bath, even if
he had to break the ice in some pond
or stream for it.

Moreover, there were times when his
tireless cheerfulness and strength seemed
discordant and untimely. When you
have been marching all day loaded like
a pack mule with knapsack, haversack,
canteen, cartridge-box, and gun ; when
every bone aches and every nerve is
unstrung, it becomes an added bitterness to have in the ranks a mere boy
whose vitality rises in jest and song
above the common misery of stalwart

men. At such times I have heard men swear at Joe with deep and apprehensive curses which showed that they felt him a little uncanny.

But I knew him as few others did. A kinder tent-mate no man ever had; my heart melts even now when I recall his unvarying gentleness and consideration; how, often after a weary day's march when at last halt was called and arms stacked and fuel must be sought for the camp-fire, he would look at me with gravely compassionate eyes and say, "You take care of the duds and get the coffee-pot ready, and I'll find the wood." Which meant, "Poor worn-out comrade, take it easy and rest, and let me do the work!" — though I think he was never too tired to enjoy the charge on the nearest fence and the scrimmage for the often too scarce rails. And always in all our rude housekeeping he would take to himself more than his share of the heaviest tasks. It was beautiful also to see his devotion to his absent father, between whom and himself an affectionate comradeship existed which was none too common in those days. His letters, almost all of them to his father, were more frequent than those of any man in the company. Much of the time he wrote daily; he used to say, "I keep my diary in this way." Under his light and effervescent manner there was strong and manly thoughtfulness which showed itself even in his jests. One of these is worth recording, not only as illustration of his originality, but for its inherent wisdom and its epigrammatic form.

On the march through the Virginia hill country, foraging, though forbidden by general orders, became the fashion. This precisely suited Joe's enterprising disposition, and by his dashing raids upon pigs and chickens he made a name for himself in the regiment. After one of these exploits, rather bolder than usual, a comrade whose conscience was tender in such matters ventured to remonstrate with him. The Suspension of the Habeas Corpus Act was just then a subject of agitating discussion throughout the country and the camps, and I shall never forget either the finely simulated sternness or the remarkable adaptation of Joe's crushing reply to his scrupulous friend.

"See here! Don't you know that war is a suspension of the Ten Commandments?"

We could not but feel that there was something more than ordinary in this boy; yet even his few intimates — those who thought they knew him — were scarcely prepared for the revelation of his character which was to come with the test of battle.

On the day when we stormed the

Marye's Hill, after we had gained the crest and the foe was fleeing before us, we pushed on through the woods that crowned the height until we came suddenly upon an open space dotted with the stumps of trees that had been felled for Confederate camp-fires. On the other side of this opening were two guns, the section of a battery which our enemies had hastily drawn up in a brave attempt to check our advance, and our captain had scarcely time to shout, " Lie down, quick ! " before a volley of grape-shot whizzed and hummed about us and laid several of our men low. The lieutenant-colonel called for volunteers, and a thin and hasty skirmish line disappeared among the stumps. Another volley of grape and another came, and then, far to the front, more than half way between us and the enemy two rifle shots rang out, and the captain of the battery fell. The gunners, apparently dismayed at the loss of their commander and at such near and mysterious foes, hastily limbered up their pieces and hurried them away. We were as much astonished and mystified as they, until presently Joe, and a companion from another regiment whom he had picked up, rose from among the stumps and came sauntering into the line. Those two bold fellows had slipped out beyond the skirmish line, and, eyeing the enemy's guns like cats, they had dropped behind the stumps as soon as they saw the gunners about to fire ; then, when the grape ceased rattling about them, up again and half running, half creeping, they had thus worked their way forward until they were within fifty yards of the battery ; then, watching their chance both aimed together at the captain and brought him down.

The colonel thanked Corporal Joe

before the regiment for silencing the battery, and that was all the reward he received, or indeed cared for.

Absolute fearlessness is rare. Perhaps it does not exist in the heart of a sane man. The bravest are usually like our heroic lieutenant-colonel, who, when an officer said to him one day, "Colonel, you don't seem to know what fear is," replied in his abrupt way, —

"All a mistake. I am always afraid, miserably afraid, whenever I go into battle, but of course it would never do to show it!"

Yet there are exceptional characters for whom the voice of the battle siren possesses irresistible fascination, — men whose overmastering delight in danger seems to scare their very fears and send them slinking away to hide in some obscure corner of their souls. After our days at Marye's Hill and Salem

Heights, we began to see such a man in
Joe, and from that time onward his
career, which was marked by a con-
tinued series of daring exploits, con-
firmed the judgment.   Moreover, it
was characteristic of the man that his
peril-defying deeds were never the result of any rage of battle.   They were
always either deliberately planned, or
else the quick and cool acceptance of
some desperate chance.

It was my good fortune to be with
him in one of the mildest of these
adventures.   After the brilliant affair
at Franklin's Crossing just before the
northward march of the army toward
Gettysburg, our regiment was sent out
beyond the captured earthworks as
skirmishers.   Night was coming on by
the time our line was established, and
we found ourselves in a romantic but
risky position.

We were occupying the grounds of

the old Bernard House. Across the broad driveways and once pleasant lawns and gardens, now neglected and weed-grown, we Northern invaders had stretched our picket line. Just behind us, its ruined and fire-stained walls touched with the mystery of moonlight, lay all that was left of the once proud mansion. In days not so very long gone by, on just such nights as this, those hospitable halls and the noble grounds had been alive with the festive gathering of Virginia's wit and beauty. Their spirits seemed to haunt the scene, so silent now save for the low-toned orders and warnings of our officers. In front of the ruined mansion stood a grove of ancient and noble oaks. They served to hide us, but they were not to be trusted. They also furnished a dangerous screen through which the enemy might easily come upon us unaware. So the lieutenant-colonel evidently thought, for he came to our company and asked quietly for half-a-dozen volunteers to act as scouts.

I think the colonel came to our company because he knew Joe was there, and he instantly responded. But I have often wondered at the strange impulse which seemed to compel me and the others to step forth by his side. After the men once knew him, Joe never went begging for followers; there was an irresistible infection in his example, and an allurement in his cheerful fearlessness that not only made men forget peril, but made it seem a privilege to go with him. It was so afterward in affairs compared to which our adventure of that night was but a pleasure trip.

The colonel himself led us out to the further edge of the grove, posted us in couples behind trees, and gave us our instructions which were, " Watch carefully for any signs of the enemy. Their picket line is out there somewhere in front of you ; if you see any movement do not fire, but come in quietly and report, and in any case come in quietly at daybreak."

He left us ; we heard his retreating footsteps until he reached the line, and then we began to realise the situation. We were between two possible and quite probable fires. It was bright moonlight ; our regiment as we afterwards discovered, was perilously advanced and isolated ; if by any chance the enemy knew our position there would be every temptation to attack, and, if that happened, even if they should advance their skirmishers, we scouts would certainly catch it from both sides, and the worst danger was from our own men. Very few of them would know we were outside the line, and it was wholly unlikely that we could "come in quietly and report" without having a hundred rifles levelled at us. When we did come in at daybreak one of us narrowly escaped death at the hands of a comrade in his own company, who, in the gray light, mistook him for a "Reb" and tried to shoot him. The colonel knew we were likely to be sacrificed, and therefore his call for volunteers.

But Joe was in his element. "This is bully!" he exclaimed, as he surveyed the scene when we were left alone. "No officers will bother us here to-night; they think too much of keeping their precious skins whole to stir outside the line."

The prospect was certainly fascinating. Behind us the giant oaks through whose shadows the moonbeams sifted their uncertain rays; before us a sweet expanse of pale-green meadow, weird with the mingled effect of tenuous curling mists and moonlight, shot across here and there with mysterious hedge-rows and indistinct tree clumps, the possible and as we found in the morning, the actual cover of the foeman's skirmishers — a strange combination of peaceful beauty and lurking death.

The sounds too, which came to us through the still and misty air were full of ominous significance. Through the dark of the grove, the anxious but subdued voices of our officers patrolling the line, keeping the wearied pickets awake and watchful; beyond through the moonlight across the meadow the distant rumble from the railroad, the noise of unloading cars and loading wagons and the shouts of teamsters at the station within the enemy's lines perhaps a mile away, warning us that by morning he would be heavily reinforced.

We watched as the night wore away,

half-expecting, half-dreading what each
moment might spring upon us, but all
was as still as death in that pale field,
until some time after midnight a strange
white Shape came moving through the
mists. We watched it anxiously, perhaps at that chill hour a little apprehen-
sively, but as it drew near our fears
were banished. It was a poor old
worn-out war-horse turned loose to
die. We watched him grazing quietly
in the meadow, and then Joe's instinct
for adventure awoke.

" I say, let's go and capture that old
beast. What a lark it would be to
drive him before us into the line in the
morning and make the boys think we
had taken a prisoner ! "

"No, sir," I replied; "we don't know
where the enemy's skirmishers are, but
I for one am just as near them as I
want to be ! "

It was well for Joe that he had a

more cautious comrade with him, for
he yielded at last to the counsels of
manifest prudence; but all night long
he looked at that old white horse with
longing eyes.

We had not more than safely reached
our company in the morning before the
foe discovered himself, and the vener-
able oaks grew vocal with singing bullets; but I shall always cherish the
memory of that risky but harmless
adventure in Joe's dear company, for
he and I were soon to part.

I have often wondered if the shadow
of his fate did not even then come over
him at times! Recklessly cheerful as
he always was in the face of danger or
difficulty, there were moments when, to
me at least, he showed another mood.
In those gloomy days after the tragedy
of the first Fredericksburg, when the
issue of the great conflict seemed doubtful, he said to me one day : —

13

"You and I are young men; life is all before us, but what will our lives be worth in this country if the South succeeds? For my part I do not mean to live to see it."

We had in our company a lot of very young fellows, some of them less than eighteen years old, whose ardent patriotism and willing courage and endurance shamed many of their elders. We were talking one day about the readiness of these bright boys to face death and danger, when Joe said very solemnly:

"Yes! the more a man's life is worth, the less he cares for it."

A year had passed since our summer night's adventure under the oaks, and Joe had been made a commissioned officer in another regiment. Men of ours, whose time had expired, flocked to him to re-enlist under his command, and his company was largely composed of old comrades. His next real service

was in that memorable and bloody siege
of Petersburg.   I met him once during
the winter; he had been at home on
furlough and I have always suspected
that he came away with a heart wound,—
the only wound he ever received until
he met his death.   We were boys when
first we were thrown together, and bash-
ful about such things, and intimate as
I afterwards became with him he was
always reticent about his love-affairs;
but I had a feeling that one fair girl at
home could have told why Joe returned
to his perilous duty robbed of that light-
heartedness which used to diffuse itself
about him like an atmosphere.   Was it
that, or was it the gloom of the apparently endless conflict which had entered
his soul?   I could never be quite sure.

He told me in curt phrase all about
the position of his regiment close by
that famous redoubt to which the soldiers had given the significant name of

"Fort Hell," and then he said, "Some day, I think soon, Grant is going to break through those lines, and when he does, I am going to distinguish myself or get killed!"

Shortly after his return to the post of duty I had a letter from him which showed an exaggerated gleam of his old humour. It told of the loss of a number of his men in the incessant picket firing and of his own narrow escapes, and then contrasting my prospects with his own, he said, "As for me I am wedded to the Goddess of Liberty, and, by Jove! the old girl met me half way and gave me my shoulder-straps for marrying her. I like my spouse; though it is well I am not of a jealous disposition, for the Old Lady has now near a million husbands and is on the lookout for more!"

Then we heard of another of his

characteristic escapades. It was evident
that some change had taken place in
the disposition of the enemy's troops.
The officer in charge of the picket line
was anxious to know what this meant,
and Joe at once offered to investigate.
Taking two men with him he pretended
to desert to the enemy. The opposing lines were close together, and between them all was bare and open, so
that no secrecy could be practised.
Joe and his two companions sprang
across the trenches and ran toward the
Confederates, shouting as they neared
them, —

"Say, Johnnies, will you take deserters?" The fire ceased and the
answer came, "Yes, Billy, come on!
come right in!"

Then Joe left his two men and went
up closer for further parley.

"Johnnies, we want to come in, but
we're rather afraid of you Twenty-

second South Carolina fellows!" and the reply was, —

"Oh, you need n't be afraid, we're not the Twenty-second South Carolina, they were sent away from here yesterday. We're the Eighteenth Georgia!"

This was precisely the information he wanted, and with a little more artful parley he edged backwards, watching his chance, and then sending his men before him to their own lines, he ran back himself, reaching shelter barely in time, escaping unhurt through the storm of bullets which his baffled and enraged foes sent after him.

The great day came at last, the day of that awful assault on the Petersburg entrenchments. Joe had been on picket all night and, according to army rules would have been exempt from duty for the next twenty-four hours. But as he came in from his weary and perilous night watch, in the gray dawn he saw the preparation for the struggle and heard a call for volunteers. A "forlorn hope," an officer and thirty men, were wanted to lead the storming column and drive in the enemy's entrenched pickets. Joe at once offered himself; men were always ready to follow whither he led, and more than thirty came forward at once.

Out from the massed lines in the dim light of dusky dawn the devoted little band moved. Those who were with him said that, as they came to the picket posts, — rifle-pits with five or six men in each, — Joe would rush far ahead of his men straight up to the rifle-pit with drawn sword and imperious command.

" Throw down your arms and surrender ! "

And thus by sheer boldness he actually captured a half-dozen groups of pickets in succession, until at last his

summons was answered by a volley, and
one bullet struck him in the breast.
The wound, his first (unless it was that
heart wound), was his last and mortal.

As we, his old comrades, far from
the bloody field heard the news, we could
scarcely believe it. Death in battle was
common enough God knows, in those
dreadful days; but somehow Joe had
always seemed to bear a charmed life.
It was hard to think of him among the
slain. Yet there were many " I told
you so's," and not a few with wise wag
of prudent head declared, " It was bound
to come to Joe, he was always rash;
this time foolhardy."

But such talk was little heeded by
those of us who knew Joe. We knew
too well that even in most desperate
moments he would think with melting
heart of the brave men under his command, and take any risk to spare them.
We also knew how thoroughly he be-

lieved that audacity was the right hand
of success.   Such men are the nerve of
an army.   There never are very many
of them ; very few survive a great war,
for victories are won by their blood.
They are literally offerings upon the
altar of their country.   Under Joe's
rude jest about the Goddess of Liberty
I knew there was the feeling that his life
was devoted to the land he loved with
passionate ardour.

When the news of Petersburg came,
our old lieutenant-colonel, a grizzled
veteran who had been through most of
the great battles of the war came to me
and eagerly asked, — " Had I heard
from Joe ? "   I told him.   The tears
came into his eyes as he turned away
exclaiming, —

" My God ! Such men sacrificed ! "

Sacrifice

BROWNING in a well-known poem describes the Emperor Napoleon at Ratisbon. He is standing on a little mound watching the storming of the city by his army and waiting anxiously for the result. Suddenly

> " Out 'twixt the battery smoke there flew
> A rider bound on bound
> Full galloping — "

The rider is an aide, a mere boy; he is desperately wounded, " his breast all but shot in two," yet he conceals his hurt, he reaches the Emperor, flings himself from his horse and in proud tones announces the victory of the legions and proclaims the glory of Napoleon.

" The Chief's eye flashed : but presently
Softened itself as sheathes
A film the mother eagle's eye
When her bruised eaglet breathes.
'You're wounded !' 'Nay,' the soldier's pride
Touched to the quick, he said
'I'm killed, Sire !' and his Chief beside,
Smiling the boy fell dead."

In his account of the battle of Gettysburg General Doubleday relates an incident which, as he says, is like this one of Ratisbon. " After the fierce fight in the railroad cut on the first day of the battle, an officer of the Sixth Wisconsin approached Lieutenant-Colonel Dawes, the commander of the regiment. The colonel supposed from the firm and erect attitude of the man that he came to report for orders of some kind : but the compressed lips told a different story. With a great effort the officer said : 'Tell them at home that I died like a man and a soldier !' He threw open his breast, displayed a ghastly wound and dropped dead at the colonel's feet."

The two incidents are indeed similar but with a profound difference of tone. The note struck by Napoleon's aide is the brilliant one of glory ; that which vibrates in the Wisconsin officer's dying words is the proudly pathetic chord of *home*.

It was characteristic of our army, — nay, of our war and of both the contending armies, — Union and Confederate. Neither of us fought for conquest or for glory, but a heritage of clashing principles woven by no will of ours into the very beginnings of our nation's history, involving its very life, had come at last in our day to the inevitable and awful arbitrament of battle.

We who fought in that war were not professional soldiers : our gathered hosts, our regiments and companies

were composed of friends and neighbours, segments of the clustering homes
from which and for the sake of which
we had gone forth, and we knew always
that though far away we were not un-
watched.   In those creepy moments on
the verge of battle when amid whizz
of waspish bullets and angry echo of
skirmish rifles the grim shadow of
bloody strife rolled toward us, many a
boy would hear in his soul the voice of
his father's parting exhortation to play
the man ; many a young fellow would
say to himself, as the image of the dear
girl who shyly and tearfully bade him
good-bye rose before him, " She shall
never have reason to be ashamed of
me ; " and the husband, while his
thoughts fly far away to the home
where wife and children wait for him,
would pray, " God protect them if I
fall, but let me not disgrace them ! "

The constant question in our hearts

was, "What will the folks at home say about us?"

I have known sick men, really unfit for duty, who, when rumours of "a move" came, would keep out of the surgeon's way, and when their regiment was called into action would shoulder their rifles and drag themselves along with their comrades for fear some report that they had shirked might travel home. We fought with the feeling that we were under the straining eyes of those who loved us and had sent us forth, whose approval we valued more than life.

There was little talk about these things. We thought them in our hearts. We knew our comrades were thinking them, but only some very special or confidential occasion brought such thoughts to our lips. When "dying for home and country" is an event quite likely to happen in the way of

your ordinary duty of next week or to-
morrow, it becomes at once a matter
too trite to be interesting as a subject
of conversation, and too solemn for
common talk, with men of Anglo-Saxon
breed. Now this deep, widespread,
though seldom-spoken sentiment ex-
plains, as nothing else can, the enormous
sacrifices which were constantly and
willingly made in our war, — especially
when along with it due account is taken
of the character of our armies. By far
the largest number of enlistments were
made at the age of eighteen (which
often meant seventeen or even sixteen),
and the average age of our men was
twenty-five years. The Nation gave
its best; the dew of its youth, the dis-
tilled essence of American manhood
flowed into the armies of both North
and South. And when we who went
forth with those hosts read the statistics
which show that the death-harvest of

battle alone — to say nothing of the far larger reaping of disease and exhaustion — reached the awful figures of two hundred thousand, an indescribably solemn feeling comes over us: for we know well that it was not the easily spared who gave their lives; we know that the dreadful vintage of our battlefields was rich with the blood of the young, the bright, the brave, the promising.

Military critics may show, to their own satisfaction at least, how battles might have been fought less expensively, but the significant fact remains that, with the exception of Bull Run, which after all was but a small affair between two newly gathered and as yet unorganised armies, there was never a complete rout; there was not one decisive victory on either side; there was no Waterloo, the war ended simply by the exhaustion of the South, and the long succession of battles was fought by men who did not, who would not know when they were beaten. Lee and Longstreet and Hill; Grant, Sherman, Sheridan and Meade are names that will never look contemptible among the world's military leaders, yet the men who followed even more than the generals who led, made our war what it was.

A few instances taken from the story of regiments which I happened to know may help to make this clear. These incidents are typical of the fighting and the sacrifice which was common to both armies. None of them are really exceptional unless it be that of the First Minnesota, and even that might be paralleled in sacrifice several times in both Union and Confederate armies.

The story of the First Minnesota at Gettysburg seems almost an anachronism in this nineteenth century. It carries

one back to the heroic ages with a sug-
gestion of the Iliad or of the Spartans
at Thermopylæ.   Its truly modern
phase is the matter-of-fact manner in
which our military historians pass it by
with barest mention as a mere tactical
incident of a wholesale battle-field, and
the consequent ignorance of the American public concerning one of the most
romantic incidents of our history.

Minnesota was too young in those
days to have many native sons, and her
generous quota of volunteers was filled
with scions of that truest American
Aristocracy, the Commonwealth Foun-
ders whose motto is " Westward Ho ! "
Out of Eastern homes, scattered all the
way from Maine to Michigan, these
bold spirits had come to the North Star
State to carve careers for themselves,
and their country's call to arms met
with quick and whole-souled response.
The First Minnesota regiment was

fortunate in its commanders. Three
colonels had risen from it to the command of brigades, two of them regular
army officers under whose rigid school-
ing the regiment gained a high reputa-
tion for discipline and efficiency. But
Colville who commanded at Gettysburg,
was a typical Westerner, tall, ungainly,
with strong and homely face of the
Lincoln stamp. It is said that when
his turn for promotion came he at first
refused, thinking himself unfit; but the
moment of supreme trial showed his
mistaken modesty.

Perhaps you have seen a thunder-
cloud lie black and threatening in the
west on a sultry summer day. Slowly
it masses its lurid bulk, while you ask
yourself anxiously where and when it
will strike. So Meade and his generals,
unprepared as yet with their scattered
corps slowly arriving, watched Lee's
army on the second of July, the really

decisive day of Gettysburg; for Pickett's grand charge on the morrow was but a last desperate attempt to retrieve an already lost cause.

About four o'clock in the afternoon the marshalled storm marched forth roaring in the fury of Longstreet's tremendous assault upon the exposed line of our Third Corps, and from then until dark, along the Emmettsburgh Road, in the Peach Orchard, about Throstle's farm-house, amid the Rocks of the Devil's Den, up and over Round Top, to and fro through the bloody Wheat Field such a combat raged as the world had not seen since Waterloo.

Away at the rear, a mile behind the battle's outmost edge, on the slope of that ridge against which the storm spent itself at last, Battery C, Fourth United States Artillery, goes into position, and the First Minnesota, weakened now by the detachment of two companies for other duty, is ordered to its support. The eight companies number two hundred and sixty-two men : a slender battalion, for their dead and wounded have been left behind on a score of hard-fought fields.

Unlike many of our battles Gettysburg was fought in the open country, and from the vantage ground upon which the little regiment stood the scene of strife was spread before them in full view. With eager eyes and anxious hearts they watch the fury of the oncoming tempest. For half an hour it sways hither and thither ; the pressure upon our too extended lines is becoming fearful. Can the Third Corps men endure it ? No ; slowly, grimly, stubbornly fighting they are borne backward. There is a bad break yonder at the Peach Orchard, a very wrestle of demons about Bigelow's guns at Throstle's ; in the Wheat Field the ripening grain is sodden with the wine of that dark harvest which the Pale Reaper is gathering; he is triumphant now. The moments have counted out almost an hour of deepening disaster. The advanced guard of the storm, the wrack sent hustling before the gale, is sweeping up the slope. Around the flaming battery, past the silent solid line of the First Minnesota pours the pallid throng of wounded and of fugitives, the fragments of torn regiments, and behind it all, with awful impact, the storm advances, rolling inward like an oncoming tide. Its advancing waves are breaking at the very foot of the slope, when a new spirit appears upon the scene. Hancock has come. Without waiting for the reinforcements following at his order, he rides alone into the very vortex of the hellish din. His masterful presence is like magic. Order begins to shape itself out of the confusion, a new line of resistance is quickly patched from rallied regiments rendered hopeful by word that help is coming. But before the new line is complete, while as yet a yawning gap is unfilled, from behind a clump of trees the Confederate brigades of Wilcox and Barksdale suddenly emerge. They see their opportunity and, flushed with victory, with wild yells they charge directly at the gap in the new line. Consternation seizes every one. The gunners of the battery begin to desert their pieces; the First Minnesota is left alone. But that regiment has never been known to disobey an order, and its men stand firm. It is one of those moments big with fate whose issue can be met only by lightning-like decision and supreme sacrifice. Hancock's glance lights upon the little lonely unbroken regiment. Instantly he is beside Colville. Pointing to the advancing masses, he says, —

"Do you see those lines? Charge them!"

Colville's answer is the command, "Attention, battalion! Forward, double quick!"

Every man knew what it meant. It was a call to death, but not one hesitated. Down the gentle slope they go in perfect order, two hundred and sixty against three thousand. The Confederate line, blazing with fire is now only a short hundred yards away. The ranks of the little regiment are rapidly thinned, but they go forward faster and faster. One of them said, —

"We were only afraid there would n't be enough of us left by the time we reached them to make any impression on the enemy."

At the bottom of the slope is a little brook, its bed dry with summer heat, its banks lined with bushes. The enemy reach it first, and the rough crossing somewhat disorders their front line. Colville seizes his desperate chance: "Charge!" He roars the command, and down come the bayonets in level gleaming row, and at full run the men of the North dash straight at the faces of the astonished foe. One who saw it all says, —

"The men are not made who will stand before bayonets coming at them with such speed and such evident desperation."

The front line of the enemy recoils, breaks, its men flee backward and throw the second line into confusion. The brook's bed is empty now. Again Colville clutches the moment: "Halt! Fire!"

It is frightfully short range, the volley is feeble only in volume, for every shot tells and there is a hideous gap in the disordered brown ranks.

Then the heroes fling themselves into

the bed of the brook. It is a good extempore rifle-pit. They have but one care now, they will obey, not only the letter but the spirit of their orders, they will hold back that threatening mass while they can, and sell their lives dearly. They fire carefully, calmly, every shot meant to hit and hurt; and for a few moments longer fear of that desperate little wasp's nest in the brook holds thousands in check. But only for a few moments. The wasp's nest must be exterminated, and from the front of them, from the right of them, from the left of them, a concentrated and increasingly fatal fire rains. Fainter and fainter come the answering ring of rifle-shots from the little brook. The bed is no longer dry, it runs with blood.

But at last Hancock's reinforcements arrive. He has not forgotten his forlorn hopes. Not a regiment but

a brigade, two of them, three of them
he hurries to the rescue, and "the
First Minnesota is relieved."

Fifteen minutes ago they were two
hundred and sixty-two.   Now there
are *forty-seven* able to stand up and
be counted ! But not one is "missing."   No prisoners have been taken
from their ranks, none have shirked
or deserted.   Only one man of the
colour-guard remains, but he carries out
their gloriously torn flag in triumph.
Colville is desperately wounded, all the
field officers have fallen, only one captain is left.   Two hundred and fifteen,
out of two hundred and sixty-two, lie
along the slope or in the bloody little
brook.   This is the high-water mark
of heroic sacrifice.   General Hancock
said of it : —

"There is no more gallant deed in
history.   I was glad to find such a
body of men at hand willing to make

the terrible sacrifice that the occasion demanded. I ordered those men in because I saw that I must gain five minutes' time. Reinforcements were coming on the run, but I knew that before they could reach the threatened point, the Confederates, unless checked, would seize the position. I would have ordered that regiment in if I had known that every man would be killed. It had to be done."

One might have thought the First Minnesota extinguished. Far from it. At nightfall the two outlying companies came in, and with the forty-seven survivors a miniature battalion was formed in command of the brave surviving captain. On the eventful morrow, the day of final victory, the First Minnesota was again in the thick of the storm where the topmost waves of Pickett's charge spent their fury. And as though conscious that com-

mon work was no longer fit for them,
they bore themselves with exaltation.
A shot cut away the staff of their
precious colours and killed the last
man of the colour-guard. Instantly
the standard was seized by another
hand and borne far forward into the
thick of the fight; a flag was wrested
from the enemy, and after the battle
their shattered staff was spliced with
the captured one. But their captain
and sixteen good men were added to
the roll of sacrifice.

One reason why such an exploit as
that of the First Minnesota is not
better known, is that sacrifices only a
little less extreme were all too common in our war, and upon both sides.
Colonel Fox, in his carefully compiled
book on " Regimental Losses," gives
a list of sixty-four Union regiments,
and a similar and equally gruesome
one of Confederates, who suffered

losses in single battles ranging from eighty to fifty per cent of their number, and he remarks that these frightful sacrifices are not those of massacres or blunders, but such as were met with in hard stand-up, give-and-take fighting.

Now a loss of thirty per cent is considered severe, and forty per cent extreme, in modern warfare.

The gallant British Light Brigade which Tennyson's noble poem has made immortal went into their famous charge at Balaklava six hundred and seventy-three strong. Their loss was two hundred and forty-seven, or not quite thirty-seven per cent. None the less do they deserve the crown which genius has given them. They were as truly martyrs to duty as though every one had fallen.

The severest regimental loss in the war between France and Germany fell upon the Sixteenth German Infantry at Mars-le-Tour.   Forty-nine per cent of their number were killed, wounded, or missing.   But the German regiments are three thousand strong, comparable only to our brigades.   And this sacrifice of the brave Germans brings to mind the strikingly similar one of my old comrades of the Vermont Brigade at the battle of the Wilderness.

Brigades in our army were commonly composed of half-a-dozen regiments more or less, often from widely separated States; but there were exceptions. The Sixth Army Corps would scarcely have known itself without the Jersey Brigade in its first division, and the Vermont Brigade in its second.   Both became famous, and their integrity as exclusively State organisations was broken only once, when for nearly a year the regiment in which I served was brigaded with the Vermonters.   It was not a kind or judicious act on the part of the military authorities to assign us thus, but I shall always think it a piece of good fortune that I once marched and fought with those Green Mountain men, and friendships made among them are cherished still.

The brigade was like a great family whose consciousness of proud and romantic traditions and whose singular cohesiveness reminded one of the Scottish Clans. But its material was most thoroughly American. The men had the qualities of mountaineers, their reserve, independence, and resourcefulness, and among the officers were men of high character and culture, some of whom, like Senator Proctor, have since become distinguished in civil life.

Stalwart fellows those Vermonters were; above the average in both intelligence and stature, tireless on the march, cool, bitter, and persistent fighters.

At well named Savage's Station, one
of their regiments had been badly cut
up in an affair which did highest credit
to its grit and discipline, but at the
time when we were with them the
brigade as a whole had become noted
rather for losses inflicted on the enemy
than for those suffered. None who
saw and shared in it, can ever forget
their wonderful fight at Bank's Ford,
where at surprisingly small cost to
themselves they repulsed and fearfully
punished Early's Confederate division
and saved the Sixth Corps from black
disaster.

But such reputations were perilous
in our army. The demand for sacrifice was sure to reach men like these.
A year and a day from the time when
they threw off Early's flank attack at
Bank's Ford, the Vermonters found
themselves in the midst of the bloody
storm-centre of the most weird, con-

fused, and difficult of the battles of the
Army of the Potomac.

" The Wilderness " is a region the
like of which can be found only along
the Southern Atlantic seaboard. For
miles, abrupt ridges of clay or gravel
cut with ragged ravines are covered
with dense growth of woods and
brush; now scraggy oak, now hedge-
like thickets of dwarf pine, — a gloomy,
intricate, intractable region.

But its very difficulties were Lee's
advantage. His men knew the Wilderness; many of them had grown up
within it or on its borders. His plan
of battle was simple, daring, and full
of peril to his foes.

The road southward from the Fords
of the Rapidan by which Grant's army
was compelled to move leads through
this region. In the midst of the forest
the north and south road is crossed by
two others running nearly east and

west. Down these intersecting roads
Lee poured his columns, striving to
strike the dangerously extended Union
line in flank, break it into fragments,
and while entangled in the Wilderness
play havoc with it.

At the most important of these road-
junctions, at the vital point of the
Union line, the position which must be
held at any cost, on the afternoon of
the fifth of May Getty's Division of
the Sixth Corps was posted with the
Vermont Brigade in front. They
await the arrival of Hancock with the
Second Corps, hoping then to push the
enemy, now retarded in their advance
by skirmishers and by the difficult
nature of the ground, away from the
danger-point, back into more open
country where more even battle can
be had. General Grant grows impatient; he orders Getty to attack at
once without waiting for Hancock.

The narrow road is the only place
where artillery can be used. It is
occupied by a battery; the infantry
brigades must feel and fight their way
through the thicket on either side.
Suddenly the opposing lines meet.
Volleys leap like sheaves of lightning
from the brush, men fall by scores,
there are charges and counter-charges;
but in that Wilderness maze where
foes phantom-like appear and disappear the bayonet is useless. The
battle settles down to a grim trial of
endurance. To stand up is death;
the opposing lines, only a few yards
distant from each other, lie down and
fight close to the ground. Neither can
advance, because neither will give way.
The men of the South, on their native
heath, taking advantage of every foot of
familiar ground, creeping up here or there
where smallest advantage appears, are
bent on hewing a path to the Brock Road.

The Vermonters, upon whom now the weight of the battle is falling, will not yield an inch. Then was seen the close clanship of those men of the Green Mountains. Like brothers their five regiments stick together, each ready to help each without confusion, with quick comprehension of every emergency, cool, desperate, deadly in the blows they give a common enemy. But their ranks are melting mournfully in the savage heat of the weird combat; from the Vermont officers especially the Southern rifles are taking ghastly toll; for while the men fight lying down, the officers must be on their feet moving from place to place along the line. One who was there with them says, "One after another of the officers fell not to rise again, or was borne bleeding to the rear. The men's faces grew powder-grimed and their mouths black from biting cartridges; the musketry silenced all sounds, and the air of the woods was hot and heavy with sulphurous vapour; the tops of the bushes were cut away by the leaden storm that swept through them."

For two horrible hours this went on, until the arrival of the advanced division of the Second Corps brought relief. Fresh troops were sent in to hold the road, and the Vermonters were ordered to withdraw. This was easier said than done. Each side was holding the other as in a vice. Finally a daring but costly charge by one regiment, concentrating the enemy's fire upon it alone, made possible the retirement of the others in good order. The Vermont Brigade had held the road until reinforcements made it secure for that day at least, but at frightful cost. "Of five colonels of the brigade only one was left unhurt. Fifty of the best line officers were killed or wounded; a thousand Vermont soldiers fell that afternoon."

Darkness closed the battle for that day, but night brought little rest. The wounded had to be sought — too often vainly sought in the dark amid the thickets; from suspicious skirmish lines frequent gleam and rattle of nervous, fitful volleys flashed, startling the darkness, and at the dawn of day the battle opened with renewed fury. Again the bereft and decimated brigade was called to perilous and responsible duty, which they nobly fulfilled; and when the second evening came, they could count their total loss. Out of less than twenty-eight hundred who had gone into battle over twelve hundred had fallen, among whom were three-fourths of the officers on duty. The greater part of this loss fell within the two hours of the first day's fight in the woods.

It was then that the colonel of the Second Regiment was wounded, went to the rear, had his hurt dressed, returned to his post, and as he went along the line speaking words of cheer to his men was struck by a second bullet and instantly killed. His place was taken by the lieutenant-colonel, "a boy in years but of approved valour," who also was presently stricken down with a death wound, leaving the regiment without a field officer. It is worth noting that these two young officers both rose from lieutenancies to the command of their regiment, and both came out of those choice homes in which more than almost anywhere else on earth culture and conscience meet. They were sons of New England ministers. The faces of some of those fallen Vermonters rise before me to-day. There was the colonel of the Sixth, in whose regiment, along with a few comrades, I found my-

self at the time of the final onset of the
Confederates at Bank's Ford. A thrill
of admiration always goes through me
whenever I think of the superbly calm
courage with which he held us down in
the sunken road in face of that charging
whirlwind which, had it reached us,
would have swept us away like chaff.
I can hear his voice even now, as when
the foe was almost upon us it rang out
above the noise of battle in clear command, " Rise! Fire!"

Alas, he was one of the Wilderness
victims: a Christian gentleman, rever-
enced and beloved by his men and fel-
low-officers. And the captain of that
company whose line we lengthened, he
too met a pathetically heroic death.
Early in the afternoon's fight in the
woods he received a severe wound in
the head: a wound which, as one of his
comrades told me, was more than enough
to have sent most men out of the battle.

His men all loved him, and they begged him to go to the rear and have his hurt cared for. But with the blood streaming down his face, and the anger of battle in his strong soul, he sternly refused, saying, " It is the business of no live man to go to the rear at a time like this ! " A few moments later, and again he was struck by a bullet in the thigh. He retired a short distance, took off his sash, bound up his second wound, returned to his place in the line, and while cheering his men a third bullet found this hero's heart and silenced his voice forever.

The sacrifice of the Vermont Brigade was not one of numbers only. Ghastly incidents abounded in that Wilderness battle-field. One of them, told me in a letter from a Fifth Corps comrade, is unique in its horror. He was severely wounded, and, finding himself useless on the line of battle, tried to make his way to the rear. After several narrow escapes from capture, he came to a little open field. Here a number of others, like himself wounded, were gathered, and faint from loss of blood and from hunger they sat down together and tried to eat a little from shared rations of such as had any.

The little field, scarce a hundred yards across, had been the scene of conflict earlier in the day, and hundreds of dead and mortally wounded lay scattered about it.

Close by where they sat down lay a young soldier from a Connecticut regiment, frightfully shot in the breast so that his lungs protruded. His life was slowly, painfully ebbing away.

My friend and his comrades, forgetting their own hurts at the sight, tried to do what they could for him. They raised him up, put a blanket under him, and propped him against a tree so that he could breathe a little easier. By feeble motions he made them understand that he wanted something from his pocket. They searched and found a photograph of some loved one at home, which he eagerly grasped with both hands and held before his dying eyes while big tears rolled down his cheeks. But he seemed satisfied, he wanted nothing more, and my friend and his companions moved away to a little distance where they could eat their lunch undisturbed by the gruesome sight of the mangled dying man.

Presently a Georgian strayed into the field. He was wounded in the toe and was making a terrible fuss about it, limping along and using his musket for a crutch, but he stopped now and then to search the bodies of the dead for plunder. There were such ghouls, a few of them, in both armies. He came to the young Connecticut soldier; they

could see him snatch the picture from
the dying man's hands, they heard a
smothered exclamation which sounded
like, " Oh, don't!" and then they saw
the brute strike the dying man with the
butt of his musket.

My friend, who was an officer, sprang
to his feet, wounded as he was, and
emptied his revolver at the man, who at
the first shot took refuge behind the
tree.   Then the officer called for a
loaded musket, and a singular duel began, the villain behind the tree and my
friend in the open exchanging shots in-
effectually, when the Georgian, reloading
in nervous haste, sprang his ramrod. It
flew out of his hand and fell just out of
reach.   Unwilling to expose himself he
clawed for it with his musket barrel, but
in vain.   At this juncture another
wounded Confederate wandered into
the horrible little field.   He had not
seen the prelude, he saw only a com-

rade in trouble, and going boldly to his help was about to hand him his ramrod; but from a dozen mangled men still able to handle a rifle threatening voices warned him to desist and let the two have it out alone. A few more wild attempts to hook the rammer toward him, and then in desperation he suddenly lunged his body toward it. My friend says, " He looked at me sideways with a scared look, as he reached out, but I just laughed to myself and fired. He fell dead, and I fainted and knew no more till I found myself in the hospital."

The road from the Wilderness leads straight to Spottsylvania. Mere localities, lonely, obscure, faintly marked on the maps they were and are still. Yet once, for just eight days their slumber was broken by the reverberations of continuous gigantic battle; and scarcely another week in modern history has borne such fruitage of sacrifice. Official reports, which seldom err by excess, tell us that our army lost 36,000 men during those eight days. What the South lost no one knows, for General Lee had issued a special order forbidding his officers to keep the count. But figures after all are an inane expression of such an immolation. These were *men* who fell,— young men, our best. After that week and after Cold Harbor, which quickly followed, the Army of the Potomac, the generous host of volunteers for home and country's sake, was never the same.

One regiment always comes to mind when Spottsylvania is named. It is indeed only one out of many distinguished for heroic losses; but I knew it well. Its members were fellow-citizens from my own State; the regiment entered service at the same time with our own. We marched together in the Sixth Army

Corps; our first battles were alike; we both left our dead on the plains below Fredericksburg and at bloody Salem Heights.

The Fifteenth New Jersey was a choice regiment recruited from the flower of the manhood of the northern counties, and peculiarly full of that high sentiment which consecrated patriotism in 1862. It was officered largely by promotions from the veteran Jersey Brigade to which it was assigned, and after it took the field was commanded by a very able regular army officer. A light loss at Fredericksburg, a very severe one at Salem Church, where the regiment though as yet unseasoned bore itself with a steadiness and gallantry that excited general admiration, then a year of hard campaigning with but little serious fighting, and the Wilderness was reached.

The Fifteenth entered the week of

battles with four hundred and twenty-nine men and fourteen line officers, beside field and staff. Of those eight days in the Wilderness and at Spottsylvania only one passed in which they met with no loss. During the fierce fighting on the fifth and sixth of May, though holding a responsible and exposed position, they suffered surprisingly little. On the seventh, another small loss met them on the skirmish line. They marched out of the Wilderness poorer by one sadly missed captain and perhaps twenty men.

The eighth brought the Jersey Brigade as the advance guard of the Sixth Corps to Spottsylvania. At once, with no time to rest, they were plunged into the first of that remorselessly persistent series of terrific assaults which have made the name of "The Bloody Angle" forever famous. This first was but a reconnaissance ordered by General

16

Warren to "develop that hill." For the Fifteenth it meant a charge across a treacherous morass, through timber slashings protecting and hiding the enemy's works, up to and over the very parapet, then back again; and it cost them over a hundred good men. The ninth brought duty on a perilous skirmish line, with a loss which included their colour-serjeant, killed by the same sharpshooter who slew General Sedgwick, the beloved commander of the Sixth Corps. The tenth, another battle again before the Bloody Angle, and another severe loss. The modest narrative of the regiment's historian says of May 11th :—

" There was musketry firing through the early morning, and several times the roll of discharges rose high, but we were left in quiet for several hours and made up our regimental reports. Then three brigades, including our own, were ordered

to hold themselves in readiness for a
charge, and were drawn up in order.
During the night the enemy had made
their fortification in our front most
formidable. We looked up at the
frowning works and flaunting battle-
flags and felt that the attempt to capture them would be a march to death."
But the assault was postponed and "the
day was one of comparative quiet," and,
for a wonder, a day of no losses for the
Fifteenth regiment.

Seven days of ceaseless battle have
now reduced the regiment by nearly one-
third. Less than three hundred men
remain in the ranks. It has been moreover a week of pitiless, unbroken strain,
of wearing anxiety, of sleepless nights
passed in worrying marches or in nervously exhausting picket duty close to
the lines of an alert enemy. Imagine
if you can seven days and nights with
scarce a moment's respite from the

crack of cannon or the threatening rattle
of musketry, seven days when you are
seldom out of sight of the swollen
corpses of the dead or out of hearing of
the wails of the wounded ; seven horrible
days, only one of which has gone by without seeing from half-a-dozen to a hundred of your comrades shot down, and
ask yourself how fit you would be to
take part in a desperate assault, a verita-
ble march to death on the morrow?

Yet with this preparation and this
anticipation thousands of men lay down
in the chilling rain that night to get
what rest they could. An officer whom
I know well — he came home in command of the regiment — told me that
on this night he and three others, two
captains and two lieutenants, were huddled together under a shelter tent, trying to get a little rest and escape from
the pitiless storm. One of the captains,
seeing troops filing by, spoke up :

" Well, there goes the Second Corps ; we are in for another fight to-morrow, and it will be a nasty one. But I feel as though I would come out all right. I don't believe the bullet is yet moulded that will kill me ! "

The other captain replied sadly, " I don't feel that way. I do not believe I shall be alive to-morrow night."

The two lieutenants said nothing ; they only listened and thought.

Before the next night both the captains lay dead on the field, their bodies riddled with bullets, one of the lieutenants had a leg shot off and a shoulder shattered. The fourth of the group, who told me the story, escaped with a bullet-hole through his coat.

The 12th of May was ushered in with a tremendous assault by the whole of the Second Army Corps, led by Hancock. The assault was at first a sweeping success, but inside the captured work another entrenchment was encountered behind which the Confederates massed their forces, and then the real combat of the day began. It is an old story; we have all heard how the armies, locked in deadly embrace, fought hand to hand so that several times during the day the trenches had to be cleared of the dead to give foothold for the living, and how great oak-trees were actually severed by riddling bullets so that they fell as if cut down by a woodman's axe.

The morning was not far gone before all our army was engaged either within the salient, or in attempts to relieve the pressure there by fresh assaults on other portions of the line. In one of these the Fifteenth regiment met its culminating sacrifice. At one side of the Bloody Angle was an earthwork as yet untried by assault. Let us take a peep at it. To do so we must first force our way through a belt of dense pine thicket full of dead branches that tear clothes and flesh. At the edge of the thicket we come upon an open space. It is perhaps two hundred yards wide. Look across! At the farther side you see first a row of abatis — trees felled with their branches pointing outward and toward you, trimmed to sharpened points, and if you could examine closely you would find many fiendish " foot-locks" cunningly made to catch and trip any one trying to force his way through this savage fence. Beyond the abatis and above it rises a yellow earth-work, the top laid in logs, with the top-most log raised a few inches so that the defenders can fire through without ex-posing themselves. Here and there you see the muzzles of cannon gaping through embrasures, arranged in angles to sweep the open field with flank fire. The horrible, the hopeless task of the Jersey Brigade, with the Fifteenth regiment in the lead, is to capture that earthwork. The attempt seems hopeless, but attack, attack everywhere is the word to-day; no joint in the enemy's harness must be left unsmitten. Spottsylvania was not a place where only easy things were tried.

It is ten o'clock now, and within and around the Bloody Angle, at every point but this, an inferno of strife is roaring. The order comes, the regiment forces its way through the pine thicket, straightens its line as it emerges, and the earthwork bursts into flame. A bold dash now across the shot-swept open, no firing, the bayonet only, and with thinned ranks the abatis is reached. To men who march to death it is less formidable than it seems, desperate hands quickly tear it aside; up now Fifteenth, what is left of you, up the bank over the logs, inside and hand to hand, foot to foot in deadly mêlée

It is often said that the bayonet was a mere appendage in our war. But it was freely used at the Bloody Angle. The Fifteenth forced their way into that earthwork at the bayonet's point, held their costly capture for a short space, took about a hundred prisoners and a battle-flag. But too few of them were left to stand against the gathering force poured in on the little band from the inner line, and a battery is now sweeping down the brigade with flank fire of grape-shot. The order comes to retire. It is almost as perilous as the going in, and when the regiment is re-formed less than a hundred can be counted. But at nightfall others who have remained all day among the dead and wounded, entrapped as it were, creep in, and at roll-call next morning it is found that one hundred and fifty-three men and four line officers remain, out of the four hundred and

forty-four who marched into the Wilderness ! The muster-out roll of that
regiment carries the names of one
hundred and twenty-two men who
were killed or died of their wounds
in those eight days of battle. And one
hundred and sixteen of them met their
death at Spottsylvania. The heroic
chaplain of the regiment says of their
last assault : —

" We were engaged a single half
hour, but there are times when minutes
exceed in their awful bearing the weeks
and years of ordinary existence. Forty
bodies, or nearly one-fifth of the whole
regiment, lay on the breastwork, in the
ditch, or in the open space in front.
Numbers had crept away to expire in
the woods, and others were carried to
the hospital, there to have their suffer-
ings prolonged for a few more days
and then to yield their breath. The
brave, the generous, the good lay

slaughtered on the ground of our charge — the most precious gifts of our State to the sacred cause of our country."

In his " History of the Second Army Corps," General Walker says of the havoc made in that splendid organisation by the first few months of the last Virginia campaign : —

" More than twenty officers had been killed or wounded in command of brigades; nearly one hundred in command of regiments; nearly seventeen thousand men had fallen under the fire of the enemy, and among these was an undue proportion of the choicest spirits. It was the bravest captain, the bravest serjeant, the bravest private who went farthest and stood longest under fire."

That was always the story, true not once but many times, and in spirit if not in precise detail of all the battle-wasted corps of our army. As the living image of those choice spirits comes back to memory, — and some of them were my dear friends, — a significant picture weaves past and present together in imagination. Shadowy forms begin to shape themselves : they are phantoms of men in mature vigour, fitter than most of us who survive, and readier to go farthest and stay longest under the fire of that unending battle by which all true progress of our national life must be conquered. And then the picture slowly fades until only a great *vacancy* is left!

For no one need tell us who knew these men that theirs was but brute courage, only the product of military discipline. Seldom has conscience been so large a factor in war, Anglo-Saxon conscience at that, which strikes hard and gives all. The ghastly losses were no accident.

Was the sacrifice worth while? We

are far enough away from it now to look back calmly and answer solemnly, Yes !

There is a keeping of life that is its loss, and a giving of it that is largest, truest gain. The one great inconsistency of our Republic was wiped away, as alone it could be, in blood; one single dangerously-dividing controversy was forever settled by that war. The pledge of our nation's indivisibility is the precious possession of those myriad graves, and the harbinger of our growingly beneficent greatness among the nations of the earth is the power of sacrifice for high principle, to which they bear their silent, their pathetic, but ever-present testimony.

To-day, after thirty years, the fruition of the sacrifice is seen. We behold the mighty uprising of a veritably united people in the cause of humanity, and on the heights of Santiago we see men of the South standing shoulder to shoulder with men of the North, mingling their blood victoriously under the old Flag, while the world looks on with admiration not unmixed with fear.

www.ingramcontent.com/pod-product-compliance
Lightning Source LLC
Chambersburg PA
CBHW031345020726
47499CB00005B/1408